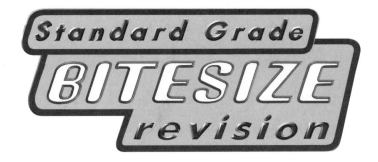

Every effort has been made to trace the copyright holders of the material used in this book. If, however, any omissions have been made, we would be happy to rectify this. Please contact us at the address below.

How to Vote leaflet courtesy of HMSO (p57); Castle definition courtesy of Macmillan (p57); *The difference a day made: Jazzie B* article courtesy of Guardian Newspapers Ltd. (p59); *Easy pickings on the street* article courtesy of *Which?* magazine (p60); *Is it fair to put Mum in a home?* article courtesy of *Woman* magazine (p62); *Queen, 71, bemoans trials of modern life* article courtesy of Guardian Newspapers Ltd. (p63); extract from F. Scott Fitzgerald, *The Great Gatsby* courtesy of Penguin Books (p64); Savoury Eggs recipe taken from *Student Grub*, published by Clarion Press and courtesy of Jan Arkless (p67); SSPCA advert courtesy of SSPCA (p67); toaster safeguards courtesy of Kenwood (p67); *Now she's old enough to look after her own smile* advert courtesy of Greater Manchester East Education & Training Consortium (p67); *Action For Blind People* letter courtesy of Action for Blind People (p68); Oxfam advert courtesy of Oxfam (p69); *How Green Are You?* article courtesy of *BBC Vegetarian Good Food* magazine (p71); *Ninja Peril of Black Lake* article courtesy of Manchester Evening News (p71); SSPCA advert courtesy of SSPCA (p72); *Adopt a Humpback Whale* courtesy of International Wildlife Coalition Trust (p73); Rhino Adoption Papers courtesy of WWF (p73); *Hi-tech, low-life* article courtesy of Guardian Newspapers Ltd (p78); *Gee, Mom, TV has made me American* article courtesy of *Daily Mail* (p79); *New Lanark Today* advert courtesy of New Lanark Conservation Trust (p82); Seamus Heaney poems – *Digging, The Early Purges, Mid-term Break, Follower* and *Storm on the Island* courtesy of Faber and Faber (p90-1); Liz Lochhead poems – *The Choosing* courtesy of Polygon, *Kidspoem/Bairnsang* courtesy of Penguin and *Box Room* courtesy of Polygon (p91-2); Siegfried Sassoon's poem, *Attack*, courtesy of Faber and Faber (p93).

Photographs: p30 courtesy of George Sutherland; p67 courtesy of Luke Finn; p69 courtesy of Oxfam.
Line drawings by Malena Stojic.

Published by BBC Educational Publishing,
BBC White City, 201 Wood Lane, London W12 7TS
First published 1999
© Trevor Gamson, Imelda Pilgrim, Marian Slee, George Sutherland/
BBC Worldwide (Educational Publishing) 1999

ISBN: 0563 46491 7

Printed by Bell & Bain, Scotland

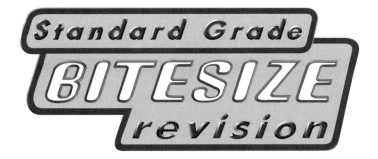

English

Based on an original text by Trevor Gamson, Imelda Pilgrim and Marian Slee with Belinda Schofield

George Sutherland

With contributions from Jenny Allan, Anne Donovan and Brian Fitzpatrick

With thanks to Jan Ainslie and Anna Muirhead

Contents

6

About BITESIZEenglish

BITESIZEenglish has been designed to help you with most of the key skills you will need for your coursework folio and the exam in Standard Grade English. It's not just a book – you can video the TV programme and access the on-line service too. There are more activities on-line and you can e-mail teachers for help. The book can be used independently or you can video the TV programmes as well.

It's called BITESIZEenglish because it's packaged in small chunks to help you learn. Most people find it much easier and more effective to study a bit at a time rather than trying to absorb everything at once. BITESIZE helps you to do this. You can watch about 15 minutes of the TV programme, then read the relevant section and try the activities. You'll have spent maybe 45 minutes working and you will have covered a whole topic. You can watch the video as many times as you want – it's a good idea to go over what you find difficult several times, then turn to the relevant section of the book.

BITESIZE isn't trying to replace your own class teacher, so you can look for help there and you can ask the on-line team to help with your questions as well. Nor does BITESIZE cover everything in Standard Grade – Talking, for example, isn't covered. However, it deals with the key parts in Reading and Writing. The literary texts it uses may not be the ones you are studying in class, but the method of learning deals with exactly the same skills, and you will learn a great deal about the poems and drama it does use. We hope BITESIZE will help you study, understand and stay in control.

About this book

KEY TO SYMBOLS

📺 A link to the video

❓ A question to answer

◎ An activity to do

This BITESIZEenglish book is divided into three main units – literary texts and then Reading and Writing for the folio and exam.

The first section in the unit on literary texts looks at Shakespeare's powerful play, *Macbeth*, and takes you through five important themes of the play. Your teacher may not have chosen *Macbeth* for the course, but it will still be useful to you. In your folio Reading tasks, you can write about texts that you have studied independently.

There are three sections on poetry. The first is on poems by the Irish poet, Seamus Heaney; the next on work of the Scots poet, Liz Lochhead; the third is on the First World War English poets, Rupert Brooke, Siegfried Sassoon and Wilfred Owen. In each of these sections, we look at the ways the poets use language to help the reader understand what they are trying to say.

There is also an important section that deals with writing about literature. This covers what you are expected to be able to do when you write the three Reading pieces on literature for your folio. It also explains why we read literature anyway. It certainly is not just for exams.

The second and third units of the book are about Reading and Writing – the close reading skills you use in the exam, and the writing skills which you need to use in both the folio and in the Writing exam. You won't find any material in the television programme for these units, but there is support on-line, and there is more material you can use in books, newspapers, magazines and all around you. Practise with this material and you will soon see how you're improving your reading and writing skills.

How this book works

Each section of the book has activities to help you. They will ask you to stop, think and carry out some tasks at the end. You learn by doing. Try to follow through with these tasks as you would for your folio. Indeed, you may want to use them for your folio. If you do, you must talk to your teacher about it. Your teacher has to be happy that it's your own work if it is going into your folio to be sent to SQA.

There are REMEMBER points (reminders) to help you as you work through the book. Read these carefully and try to use the ideas. You can make notes in the wide margins – it's your own book.

Useful words and technical terms are often **highlighted** (like this) in the book and explained in the glossary. You are supposed to be able to use these words in your writing in the folio and exams to show that you understand them. So look them up and see how they work in **context** (that's the first one).

Any sample answers that appear are just that – samples. You must write your own answers, of course, with your own point of view.

Your study plan

The students who do best plan their study over a period of time and don't try to do everything, especially "revision", all at the last minute. Most of what you do in English is not about remembering facts: it's about gaining and improving skills that help you to learn and communicate. This is not done by "revision", but by applying yourself to learning and understanding.

Much of what is in this book is needed for the folio work. Your folio is sent to the SQA at the end of March, so you have to plan accordingly. After that, however, you have to use similar skills again, and additional skills (close reading, for example) in the exam, Writing and Reading. This means that you should be using BITESIZEenglish throughout the course, not just at the time when the exams are approaching.

You should plan your time realistically. Set aside some time, not more than two hours, for study with the book, your other English work and perhaps the video. Don't try to work on for huge long periods of time: it's counter-productive. Your brain doesn't really work like that. Remember, of course, that there's not only your English to deal with. There are other subjects too.

Go back to each section more than once, after an hour or so, then a day, then a week, if you can. In this way, you'll become more familiar with the material

THE ON-LINE SERVICE
You can find extra support, tips and answers to your exam queries on the BITESIZE internet site. The address is http://www.bbc.co.uk/education/revision

and more confident. When you have drawn up a sensible plan, stick to it.

Make sure that you have good conditions for working. If you're serious about it, people will help you in this. Make sure that:

- you have a set time period in which to work
- you have a quiet place
- you've got everything you need with you – pens, paper, video, books
- you won't be distracted by music, computer games or the telephone
- you take a short break to keep you alert.

Exams and the folio

The main purpose of this book is to help you with the skills of reading and writing. Though it is not about sitting exams, you do have to sit them and you do have to complete your folio, for that is how your skills are assessed. You should have a practical strategy for your folio and exams.

Make sure that you know the deadlines for completing your folio work and that you know the date, time and place for the exams at the level (Foundation, General, Credit) you are sitting. Make sure that you arrive in plenty of time, but don't spend it panicking. You can run over important points and ideas and get yourself into the right frame of mind.

For the folio and the exam, you should make it your business to know what the requirements are – how many pieces you must write and of what kind. Your teacher will show you the folio flyleaf from SQA to give you a clear idea of the specifications for the folio. Later, you have to be familiar with which exam questions you can choose, and which ones you must attempt. The kind of answer you need is what you will learn with BITESIZEenglish.

Writing for Standard Grade

During the Standard Grade course at school, you will be given tasks and assignments in Writing and Reading. For both of these, you will produce pieces of writing. (Confusing, isn't it? The use of capital letters is the clue).

The Writing tasks will be based on any of four purposes:

- writing to convey information
- writing to deploy ideas, argue, evaluate
- writing to describe personal experience, feelings
- writing to employ specific literary forms.

The Reading tasks will be based on any of these different, but related, purposes:

- reading to gain overall impression of a text
- reading to obtain particular information

- reading to grasp ideas or feelings implied

- reading to evaluate attitudes, assumptions, arguments

- reading to appreciate the writer's craft

- reading to enjoy and obtain enrichment.

This is all said in the kind of language we call technical (polite version) or **jargon** (less approving). It is the kind of language that we will try to avoid in the book or explain in the glossary if it must be used.

There are features of your writing that will be needed whatever kind of writing you are asked to produce. These are:

Planning your work

This is always important because it shows the reader that you have thought through the whole piece, rather than just made it up as you go along. Both your teacher and the examiners will expect your work to show that it is deliberate and planned. It is almost impossible to write the final, best version straight off. Even this piece you are reading had to be planned and rewritten. Planning shows that you have thought about:

- introduction and conclusion

- what each paragraph will be about

- the order of the ideas and paragraphs.

Checking your work

When you follow your plan and complete a piece of writing, you must go back and check everything you have written. In the folio, you will, of course, have ample time to re-draft your work. In the exam, you will have time to re-draft to some extent, but you will not have time to write the whole thing out again. Don't even try.

- Look at how your sentences work.

- Is your meaning clear?

- Is your writing effective, or could it be improved by adding or removing words or sections?

- Have you really checked the spelling and the punctuation?

- Could the message be more stylishly expressed?

In each piece of writing that you produce for the folio or the exam, you must be clear about its purpose. This is why BITESIZEenglish concentrates on these purposes and the kind of writing that they demand.

We hope you enjoy working with BITESIZEenglish. Now read on... carefully.

Good luck!

This section provides advice and information that you would use in your folio reading pieces.

📺 Macbeth – the witches

When Shakespeare was writing, most people believed in witches. There were regular witch-hunts to get rid of their "evil influence". Many innocent women were accused of being witches and were burned at the stake.

◎ *Read Act 1, scenes i and iii.*

Finding the meaning

When you study the witches in *Macbeth*, you need to think about what impression they make on the audience and the influence they have on Macbeth.

Creating atmosphere

❗ REMEMBER Use a dictionary to look up any words you're not sure about.

In the short opening scene, the witches talk of a battle being lost and won, of a future meeting with Macbeth and their response to familiar spirits (Graymalkin and Paddock). In themselves, these subjects are neither frightening nor disturbing. But think about *how* the witches speak.

Contradictions

The witches speak in verse. Their lines sound like chants. They speak in riddles and paradoxes, for example, "Fair is foul and foul is fair."

This contradiction is echoed by Macbeth when he appears in Act 1, scene i:

❗ REMEMBER Try to notice themes and symbols running through the play.

So foul and fair a day I have not seen.

These contradictions introduce a feeling of opposing forces at war. They are a symbol of the struggles that take place in the play.

Foreboding

The witches create an atmosphere of foreboding. They meet in "thunder, lightning, or in rain". The air is not only "foggy" but "filthy". In just a few lines, Shakespeare has managed to create a feeling of anticipation. The audience wonders how the witches' prophecies will be borne out.

(?) *How would you produce the opening scene of "Macbeth" so that it had a strong impact on an audience? You should think about the appearance of the witches, the way they say their lines and the background setting, lighting and sound.*

10

Forces of evil

Do the witches represent evil? Look at the spells at the opening of Act 1, scene iii. The Second Witch has been "killing swine". The First Witch holds "a pilot's thumb". The evil isn't always explicit. Can you feel a sense of menace in the picture of "a sailor's wife" who "munch'd, and munch'd and munch'd"? Look how Shakespeare presents disturbing details. For example, the First Witch will change into a rat with no tail, and ominously repeats "I'll do, I'll do and I'll do".

The witches are powerful enough to control the weather ("I'll give thee a wind") and they hint at things to come:

Sleep shall neither night nor day
Hang upon his penthouse lid.

The first section of scene iii is wound up with a charm:

Thrice to thine and thrice to mine
And thrice again, to make up nine.

Influence on Macbeth

Power of prophecy

You can see one of the witches' chief dramatic functions in their meeting with Macbeth and Banquo. Notice how Macbeth and Banquo repeat the witches' words, almost as though the witches have some supernatural influence over them. Macbeth says: "So foul and fair a day I have not seen" and Banquo calls the witches "things that do sound so fair." Banquo feels that they possess powers of prophecy:

If you can look into the seeds of time,
And say which grain will grow and which will not.

The witches foretell Macbeth's future rise to power and Banquo's ability to create kings, but not become one, saying "Thou shalt get kings, though thou be none." The witches disappear and Macbeth and Banquo are left to discuss the meaning of their words. When they receive the news from Ross and Angus, Macbeth thinks about the prophecies. They seem to have sown the seed of murder in his mind, although the idea of committing murder to fulfil the prophecy begins to disturb him:

My thought, whose murder yet is but fantastical
Shakes so my single state of man that function
Is smother'd in surmise.

(?) How does Shakespeare convey a sense of evil and menace through the words of the witches?

11

Macbeth

Folio Reading Task

Look at how Macbeth and Banquo react to the prophecies of the witches.

Explain what you think is going through the minds of each of these characters at this stage in the play. Refer to the text to support your ideas.

⊤ᵥ Persuading Macbeth

◎ *Read Act 1, scene v.*

Finding the meaning

Evil intention

You could say that Lady Macbeth is evil. Such an interpretation is based on the comments she makes about the letter's contents. Notice how she criticises her husband who is "not without ambition" but doesn't want to get his hands dirty:

> What thou would'st highly
> That would'st thou holily

She regrets that he is a man of integrity who "would'st not play false".

After hearing the messenger's news of Duncan's intention to stay with them, she says she wants to change her personality. She wants to lose her femininity, saying "unsex me here", and be made of nothing but evil:

> And fill me from the crown to the toe top-full
> Of direst cruelty!

She seems determined to be the one to murder Duncan:

> That my keen knife see not the wound it makes.

Does she really relish the prospect of being a killer? Or is she steeling herself to do the deed?

? *In what ways do the following quotations suggest that Lady Macbeth has a softer side to her nature?*

- *Stop up the access and passage to remorse*
- *Nor heaven peep through the blanket of the dark*

When Macbeth appears, it is Lady Macbeth who appears to be the stronger partner. She is determined that Duncan won't leave their castle alive. She urges Macbeth to disguise his evil intentions.

◎ *Now read Act 1, scene vii.*

Macbeth's doubts

The scene opens with a **soliloquy** in which Macbeth thinks about the consequence of murder. Killing would be easy if there was to be no judgement:

> That but this blow
> Might be the be-all and end-all here.

There is, however, the judgement to come after death, and the judgement of justice in this life. There is also the problem of Macbeth's troublesome conscience:

Bloody instructions, which, being taught, return
To plague the inventor.

 Macbeth gives his reasons for not murdering the king. Make a list of these reasons. Can you place them in their order of importance?

When Macbeth discusses the proposed murder with his wife, she again appears to be the dominant partner. Macbeth wants to drop the subject:

We will proceed no further in this business.

She tries to shake him out of this attitude:

Was the hope drunk wherein you dress'd yourself?

She calls him a coward. He replies by saying he is no coward:

I dare do all that may become a man.

Lady Macbeth uses the powerful image of dashing out her new born child's brains in order to shame Macbeth. Macbeth wonders if they might fail. Lady Macbeth accepts the possibility of failure but argues that, if Macbeth is courageous, they will not fail.

She then outlines her plan. She is the practical one and finally she persuades Macbeth, who says:

I am settled, and bend up
Each corporal agent to this terrible feat.

You can view the relationship between Macbeth and Lady Macbeth in different ways. Do you think she is a dominant character leading her husband down the path of darkness? Or do you see them as a team with different strengths, working together and supporting each other?

Folio Reading Task

Look at the following two statements:

■ If Lady Macbeth had not intervened, Macbeth would not have murdered Duncan.

■ Lady Macbeth simply encouraged Macbeth to murder Duncan. He would have done it anyway.

Argue the case for each statement, referring to the text in support of your ideas.

Which argument do you think is the stronger one? Why?

⊕ The morning after the murder

◉ *Read Act 2, scene iii.*

Finding the meaning

In the previous scene, Macbeth and Lady Macbeth react in private to the horrors of the murder. Macbeth is distraught, convinced he has murdered "the innocent sleep" and that his hands will never be clean. Scornfully, Lady Macbeth reassures him that "a little water clears us of this deed". Now we see them having to react in public. They must keep up the appearance of innocence, while at the same time come to terms with their private feelings.

Changes in tone

Dramatic tone

The scene is made more dramatic by the shifts in tone. It opens with dramatic knocking.

Comic tone

The drunken porter's speech is a moment of comedy at a point of high drama. It relieves the tension for a moment, so that what follows will seem more exciting.

⁇ *What do you make of the porter's speech? Is it hard to understand? The joke about drink and lechery is obvious enough, but many of the jokes are obscure. Notice, however, the disturbing images, like "Here's a farmer who hanged himself on the expectation of plenty."*

⁇ *Jot down some examples of contradictory behaviour given by the porter. Can you find more examples in the rest of the play?*

Light tone

The porter's drunken behaviour makes Macduff and Lennox think that there has been a celebration. This lightens the tone, since the last thing the visitors would expect is that murder had been committed. When Macbeth appears, he sustains this mood with idle banter:

> Macduff: I know this is a joyful trouble to you.
> Macbeth: The labour we delight in physics pain.

Darker tone

The mood darkens with Lennox's description of the night. Nature seemed to have been at war with the Earth:

> Some say the earth
> Was feverous and did shake.

The tension reaches a new climax with Macduff's dramatic entrance:

> O horror, horror, horror!

Unintentionally, he reminds Macbeth of one of his reasons for not wishing to kill Duncan, i.e. Duncan's divine right to be king:

> Most sacriligious murder hath broke ope
> The Lord's anointed temple.

Yet Macbeth remains calm, asking innocent questions. Macduff heightens the dramatic tension by demanding an alarm bell be rung.

On her entry, Lady Macbeth plays the innocent. Macduff is convinced by her act and tries to protect her from news of the murder:

> 'Tis not for you to hear what I can speak!

When the news does break, Lady Macbeth's only concern is that it should have been committed in her house. Macbeth, however, appears deeply disturbed. He wishes he had died before the murder. The murder has apparently changed the way he thinks about life, as he says: "There's nothing serious in mortality." To Donalbain's innocent question, "What's amiss?", Macbeth replies in strong terms. After Lennox's vivid description of the murdered servants, Macbeth admits to having killed them.

Use of language

Think about the speech beginning: "Who can be wise, amazed, temperate and furious ...". What does the language tell you about Macbeth's state of mind? Why do you think he describes the murder scene in such vivid detail? Is it because of his horror at Duncan's appearance, does he think that this way he can prove his innocence, or has Macbeth been fascinated by what he has done? He says:

> His silver skin laced with his golden blood.

The richness of the language possibly indicates a morbid fascination.

It's difficult to decide whether Banquo knows who killed Duncan. His words are ambiguous. He speaks of "fears and scruples", almost as if he fears he knows who did the deed, but he has scruples in view of his relationship with Macbeth. Remember, of course, that both Banquo and Macbeth heard the witches' prophecies. Banquo certainly calls the murder "treasonous malice".

! REMEMBER
In your writing, you should show that you are aware of different interpretations of the characters' words and actions.

15

Macbeth

(?) *Lady Macbeth faints. Do you think this is a genuine reaction or is it an attempt to divert people's attention? After her dramatic faint, Malcolm and Donalbain quietly contemplate their position. Do they decide to flee from Scotland or from Macbeth? What do you think?*

Folio Reading Task

1 How do Macbeth and Lady Macbeth react to the announcement of the murder of Duncan?

2 Do you think their reactions are genuine, an attempt to fool the others, or a mixture of both? Give reasons for your answer.

Ⓣⓥ The banquet

◎ *Read Act 3, scene iv.*

In this scene, Macbeth is forced to face up to the reality of the evil he has done. First, he is responsible for the death of Duncan, king by divine authority. Now he has hired murderers to dispatch Banquo and his son Fleance, so that the witches' prophecy cannot be fulfilled.

Finding the meaning

The scene opens like any normal dinner party. Macbeth bids everyone a "hearty welcome" and says he will "play the humble host". At the murderers' news that Fleance has "'scaped", Macbeth hints that his mind is becoming unhinged: "Then comes my fit again".

❓ *Look closely at Macbeth's reaction to the news that Fleance has escaped. He feels "cabin'd, cribbed, confined". What do these words suggest? What ideas are revealed through the images of the serpent and the worm? A "brainstorm" diagram would be a good way to explore these ideas. See an example of this on page 31.*

Macbeth tries to rid his mind of doubts and turns his attention to his guests:

> Now good digestion wait on appetite,
> And health on both!

He even wishes that Banquo were at the feast. Almost as if prompted by this, Banquo's ghost takes his place at the table. Shocked, Macbeth at first puts the blame on his guests, asking "Which of you have done this?"

He addresses the ghost directly. Lady Macbeth, as she had done in the scene following Duncan's murder, tries to divert criticism:

> The fit is momentary... feed and regard him not.

Macbeth returns to his predicament which haunts him throughout the play. While he is brave on the battlefield, he finds murder unnatural:

> Ay, and a bold one, that dare look on that
> Which might appal the devil.

Lady Macbeth reminds him of his vision of a dagger that led him towards Duncan's bedchamber. Macbeth insists there is a ghost. The imagery indicates Macbeth's unhinged mind:

> Our monuments
> Shall be the maws of our kites.

Killing and burying his victims will not solve his problems. He imagines the graves spewing the bodies back into the world. Macbeth feels the dead will return to get their revenge. You can feel the horror in his words:

The time has been
That, when the brains were out, the man would die,
And there an end; but now they rise again.

Macbeth is persuaded to rejoin the guests. Notice how Macbeth wavers between normality and insanity in this scene. At one moment, he plays the host as if nothing had happened. The next he is appalled by the apparition. On the ghost's next appearance, Macbeth returns to his obsessive fear, saying that he can face any normal danger bravely ("my firm nerves shall never tremble"). To Macbeth, the ghost is so palpably present he believes his wife must see it too. It is at this point that Lady Macbeth bids their guests leave immediately, putting aside formalities:

Stand not upon the order of your going.

◎   *Imagine you were a guest at the banquet. Describe what you saw, heard and thought about these strange events.*
This would not be the kind of task for your folio. However, it is a valuable exercise in helping your understanding of this scene.

The break-up of the party is a kind of visual image of Macbeth's mental breakdown. On the guests' departure, he muses on his private fears:

It will have blood; they say blood will have blood.

He is beginning to believe in the supernatural world of the witches:

Stones have been known to move and trees speak.

In fact, he is determined to visit the witches again to confirm his worst fears. There can be no going back on his murderous intentions:

I am in blood
Stepp'd in so far that, should I wade no more
Returning were as tedious as go o'er.

Banquo's apparition has convinced him. He is now determined on his evil course, though he sees it as an inevitable and tedious one. Lady Macbeth, however, thinks there is hope, if only he could sleep. She says:

You lack the season of all natures, sleep.

Macbeth disagrees. His way ahead is more killing. It is as if he is saying they have only just begun:

We are yet but young in deed.

⚛   *Is it this – the realisation that there is more horror to come – which finally causes Lady Macbeth's insanity?*

Folio Reading Task

The banquet scene is the turning point in the play for Macbeth and also for Lady Macbeth.

Show how this event marks the point of change for each of the two main characters.

 # The end of Lady Macbeth

> ◎ *Read Act 5, scene i.*

Finding the meaning

The audience enters the nightmare world of Lady Macbeth's mind. Shakespeare uses the dialogue between the Doctor and a Waiting-Gentlewoman to prepare for her entry. When the audience sees Lady Macbeth sleep-walking, it is reminded of Macbeth's prophetic words, "Macbeth does murder sleep".

Lady Macbeth seems confused, but notice how her mind relives the key moments in her life.

> ◎ *Look at Lady Macbeth's speeches in this scene. Make a list of quotations and events from earlier scenes in the play to which she is referring.*

Her concerns reveal her state of mind now, but they also recall her former self. For example, "Yet who would have thought the old man to have had so much blood in him" is a reference to their blood-stained hands after the murder of Duncan. In the same way, the never-ending washing of her hands and her complaint: "What, will these hands ne'er be clean?" is an ironic reference to the advice she gave to her husband in Act 2, scene ii:

    A little water clears us of this deed.

Notice that in the heat of the moment, she felt their guilt would be quickly and easily washed away. Now, in her mind, she realises that she will never be able to get rid of her guilt.

She also carries the burden of her husband's fear. She is obsessed by the terror her husband felt in the banquet scene. Then he spoke of his fear that the dead would rise and "push us from our stools". She says about his dilemma:

    I tell you yet again, Banquo's buried; he cannot come out on's grave.

Her madness is conveyed in several ways. You'll have already noted that her thoughts appear to be spoken at random, but there is a kind of insane logic in them. She speaks in prose. She has rejected the fine verse of a queen's speech. All she has left is her basic humanity. She appears obsessed with key symbols of the play: blood, standing for guilt; and water, representing longed-for forgiveness. Finally, she invites pity for her condition by referring to her hand as "little".

Interpretation

Since the words are simple and the expression disjointed, you can interpret them in a variety of ways.

◉ *Read Lady Macbeth's speeches from this scene aloud. Decide how much feeling to put into them and, more importantly, how much to leave out. Test your interpretation against what you have learned about the character of Lady Macbeth earlier in the play.*

Changes in mood

◉ *Read Act 5, scene iii, after the entrance of Seyton. Also read Act 5, scene v, up to the point where a messenger enters.*

When the Doctor speaks of Lady Macbeth's "thick coming fancies", Macbeth orders him to cure her. He asks:

> Can'st thou not minister to a mind diseased,
> Pluck from the memory a rooted sorrow?

He is speaking of his wife's predicament. But is it a cry from his own heart? He, too, may be longing for "some sweet, oblivious antidote". Nevertheless, he soon dismisses that mood and dispatches physic "to the dogs".

Immediately, he becomes involved in the task of defending Dunsinane Castle. He says he has "almost forgot the taste of fears".

> Direness, familiar to my slaughterous thoughts,
> Cannot once start me.

When Seyton announces the death of the Queen though, Macbeth's mood changes. He becomes fatalistic and philosophical about the meaning of existence. Life, he says, is very brief:

> Out, out, brief candle!

A person is as insignificant as a poor actor. Personal fame is soon forgotten:

> ... a poor player
> That struts and frets his hour upon the stage
> And then is heard no more.

Life itself is meaningless, "signifying nothing".

All Macbeth has left to believe in is the witches' prophecies that he will not be defeated until "Birnam Wood do come to Dunsinane" and that he cannot be killed by anyone who is "not born of woman". His wife has been broken by the tragic events of their lives. He will survive by clinging to a belief in prophecies which, finally, prove to be false.

Folio Reading Task

In what ways are Macbeth and Lady Macbeth shown to suffer for the crimes they have committed, and for whom do you feel the greater sympathy? Explain your choice by reference to the text.

⊚ Following an argument

Seamus Heaney

This section helps you to read poems so that you can write about them in the folio. It uses the work of Seamus Heaney.

The task in a Reading piece for the folio might be to trace the **argument** of a poem. To prepare for this you should:

- **read** the poem several times
- **brainstorm** it, writing down as many points as you can

With these points in mind, go through the poem, stage by stage, to find out how the poet has presented his argument.

 Re-read and brainstorm "Digging" on page 90. Write down your points. Think about what the poet has to say directly to you.

Tracing the argument

The poem opens with a picture of the writer at work. He feels very comfortable doing what he's doing (the pen is "snug"). He also feels that being a writer makes you very powerful. He imagines his pen is a gun.

The noise of digging attracts his attention: "Under my window, a clean rasping sound". As the poet looks at his father's backside bent over the ground, he calls to mind memories of him digging and the poem shifts in time to "twenty years away".

The poet notices several things about the way his father works. He tries to capture the actual feel of digging by using **alliteration**. This emphasises the cutting edge of the spade:

 buried the bright edge deep.

Heaney uses the word "deep" to close the line cleanly and sharply – like the spade-cut. He emphasises his delight by using more alliteration:

 Loving their cool hardness in our hands.

 Re-read lines 6-15. Write a paragraph explaining how Heaney portrays his father digging.

A second major time shift takes place and Heaney starts to write, with pride, of his grandfather:

 My grandfather cut out more turf in a day
 Than any other man on Toner's bog.

The events of the poem are made more vivid by the recollection of an incident from Heaney's childhood:

Once I carried milk in a bottle

The detail he introduces makes it all the more real:

Corked sloppily with paper.

Heaney uses alliteration again to emphasise his grandfather's skill:

heaving sods
Over his shoulder

Sharp consonants are used to bring out the actual sound of the digging:

Nicking and slicing neatly.

 List the similarities in the portrayal of Heaney's father digging and his grandfather digging.

The way Heaney recreates the sounds and feeling of digging is essential, because the poet is recalling early memories. If you, as the reader, can feel what the poet felt, then you can appreciate what it meant for Heaney.

The next stanza uses **onomatopoiea** – more vivid sounds – to recreate the sounds of digging:

the squelch and slap

and:

the curt cuts of an edge.

Heaney feels he cannot follow in the family footsteps. He writes:

But I've no spade to follow men like them.

The poem comes full circle, returning at its conclusion to the poet sitting waiting to write. The pen is no longer a gun, but a spade with which Heaney decides to dig. Heaney is now in harmony with his father and grandfather.

REMEMBER
Look for what the poet suggests through the use of language – in images, symbols, rhyme and rhythm.

Seamus Heaney

Folio Reading Task

By comparing his work to the work of his father and grandfather, what do you think Heaney is suggesting about the importance of the past?

 # Understanding the issues

Poets sometimes write accounts of their experiences that reveal how they feel about the things they describe. The poets may state their **moral** viewpoint – whether they think something's right or wrong. Usually however, they suggests possibilities. When reading a poem, you have to make up your own mind.

◎ *Read and re-read "The Early Purges" (page 90) several times. The poem looks at cruelty and suffering and asks if they are a necessary part of life.*

Expressing views

Heaney uses three voices to present his point of view.

The first belongs to himself as a young child:

I was six when I first saw kittens drown.

The next voice is that of a farm worker, Dan Taggart:

Sure isn't it better for them now?

The final voice belongs to the poet as a grown man:

But on well-run farms pests have to be kept down.

The three voices express three attitudes towards cruelty:

- the young child is horrified
- Dan Taggart thinks it's just a part of farming
- the adult poet seems to recognise the practical necessities.

REMEMBER Underline words and phrases that show the poet's attitude.

❓ *Do you think the last voice is saying what Heaney actually believes?*

Using emotive language

Words which make us feel strongly about a subject are known as **emotive** words. Writers generally use them to persuade you of a particular point of view. Look closely at the language to see how the child's view is presented:

REMEMBER Watch out for emotive words and phrases. Consider the effect they have on the reader.

- a frail metal sound
- their tiny din was soon soused
- three sogged remains

- soft paws scraping like mad
- glossy and dead
- mealy and crisp

◎ *Write a sentence about each phrase.*

Now look at what Dan Taggart says. He calls the kittens "the scraggy wee shits" and asks "Sure isn't it better for them now?"

Which of the following words do you think best describe his attitude?

cruel indifferent heartless mean practical ruthless considerate

(?) *How do you feel about Dan Taggart's words and actions?*

In the fifth stanza, Heaney writes about death on the farm by simply stating what the farm labourer did ("trapped", "snared", "shot"). Notice how matter-of-fact these duties seem to be.

In the final line, however, Heaney tries to appeal to the reader's sympathies by using emotive language. He states that the "tug" was "sickening", and the hen was "old".

Next, comes the poet's adult voice. He states simply that "living displaces false sentiments". He is saying that his feelings as a young child are to be forgotten. They were "sentimental" and they prevented him from seeing the world as it really is. They were "false". It is only people in towns who think farming is cruel:

"Prevention of cruelty" talk cuts ice in town.

Reminding us of Dan Taggart, he now speaks of "bloody pups" and argues that "on well-run farms pests have to be kept down".

(?) *Does Heaney really mean this? How can you tell? Does it matter?*
Look for evidence in the poem.

Folio Reading Task

Write an evaluation of "The Early Purges" in which you identify the central issue and show the different views about this issue which are explored in the poem. You should show how Heaney uses language to influence the reader.

Reading between the lines

Poetry often deals with unfamiliar situations and feelings. Through reading a poem closely, you can learn a lot about other people's lives and experiences. Often, you have to think carefully about what lies below the surface of a poem in order to understand it fully.

◎   *Re-read "Mid-Term Break" (page 90). Remember that this poem is based on Heaney's own experience.*

Relating to unfamiliar experiences

Not everybody who reads this poem has been to a boarding school or knows what a sick bay is. Fewer still will have experienced the painful loss of a brother or sister. Nevertheless, there are many points to which we can readily relate.

Heaney's picture of school is not too far removed from life in a state-run school today. Bells ring whichever type of school you go to. What is unusual about these bells is that they are "knelling". They sound sombre, setting the mood for what is to follow.

Revealing hidden feelings

! **R E M E M B E R** Poems are seldom simply **literal**. Your Reading pieces should always show that you have thought about what lies beneath the surface message of a poem.

Lines 4-13 describe the young boy's homecoming. The only feeling described is his embarrassment at the old men standing up to shake his hand.

   How do you think the young Heaney might have felt about:
- *his father crying*
- *Big Jim Evans*
- *the baby in the pram*
- *the strangers*
- *his mother's sighs*
- *the difference between his father and his mother.*

Why do you think these feelings are not described?

There is a sense of restraint in this poem, as though the feelings are being deliberately held back, lying just beneath the surface, perhaps because they are still too difficult and too painful for Heaney to express openly. This sense of restraint is reinforced by the arrival of the body which is described in a very distant and impersonal way:

At ten o'clock the ambulance arrived
With the corpse, stanched and bandaged by the nurses.

The exact time is given and the body of his brother is referred to as "the corpse", almost as it would be in a news report.

Symbols

The final seven lines of the poem describe how Heaney went to see the body of his young brother the following morning.

(?) *Think about the following phrases:*

- *Snowdrops and candles soothed the bedside*
- *Wearing a poppy bruise*
- *No gaudy scars*

What do you associate with snowdrops and candles? What do they **symbolise***?*

Why is the bruise described as "a poppy bruise"? Is this simply descriptive or are there other connotations?

What does "gaudy" mean? Are scars normally described as being gaudy? Why do you think Heaney chose to use the word here?

Statements of fact

You have already noted how restrained the feelings are in this poem. This sense of restraint is, in part, created by the use of flat statements of fact, such as "I sat all morning in the college sick bay".

 List as many simple statements of fact as you can find in the poem.

It is only at the close of the poem that we learn, with the phrase "the bumper knocked him clear", how Heaney's brother died. This is stated simply, almost as a matter of fact. Does this mean there is no emotion behind it?

The poem finally ends abruptly with just two short phrases:

A four foot box, a foot for every year.

(?) *How effective do you find this as an ending?*

> **!** **REMEMBER**
> As a reader of poetry, you need to form your own opinions about the poet's meaning. When you write your folio Reading pieces, you should support your **personal stance** by referring to the text.

Seamus Heaney

Folio Reading Task

In "Mid-Term Break", Heaney writes about his brother's death.

How effectively does the poet bring out his feelings in the poem?

⊙ Looking at language

You must look closely at the language of poetry if you are to understand the poet's intentions. You also need to be able to:

- write about the language

- comment on its **effectiveness**.

Descriptive language

⊙ *Read and re-read "Follower" (page 90-1).*

Here Heaney is writing about his father and his relationship with him. Look at the way Heaney describes his father when he was younger:

- His shoulders globed like a full sail strung

- An expert

-                                 His eye
  Narrowed and angled at the ground,
  Mapping the furrow exactly

- Sometimes he rode me on his back
  Dipping and rising to his plod

- his broad shadow

 R E M E M B E R
Look closely at the language in order to be able to comment on its effectiveness.

Think about the first of these images. When Heaney's father is ploughing, his shoulders seem "globed like a full sail strung". The word "globed" not only suggests the way his shoulders were rounded and powerful but that they seem, to the young boy, as big and as important as the whole world. The use of the **simile** "like a full sail strung" reinforces the image of power and strength, adding a suggestion of tautness and effort.

⊙ *Look back to the list of things that Heaney says about his father. Explain what ideas each of these conveys and how Heaney achieves this through the use of language.*

Contrasting language

The image of the young Heaney contrasts sharply with the powerful images of his father.

- I stumbled in his hob-nailed wake.
- All I ever did was follow

and:

   I was a nuisance, tripping, falling,
   Yapping always.

(?) *What impression of the young Heaney is created by these words?*

His father's power and strength is not only conveyed through the descriptions of him. It is apparent also in his control of the horses and the soil. The horses "strained at his clicking tongue". This image conveys the idea that they are listening carefully and he is clearly in command. With "a single pluck" of the reins he is able to turn the horses round. The word "single" emphasises the extent of his control. The way the "sod rolled over without breaking" suggests that even the soil obeys him.

Change of tone

The last three lines of the poem take the reader by surprise. Without warning, the order is reversed. Now that Heaney is a grown man, it is his father "who keeps stumbling behind" and "will not go away". In many ways, their roles have been reversed.

(?) *Is the tone one of sadness, resentment, or a mixture of both?*
Is Heaney sorry that his father has become dependent on him?
What do the words "will not go away" tell you about Heaney's feelings towards his father?

! REMEMBER Always use evidence from the poem to support what you have to say in your writing. Do this either by **quoting** or by **referring** to it.

Use of rhyme

The neat rhymes "sod/plod" emphasise the neat cuts his father makes with the plough. There are also several examples of half-rhyme:

■ plough/furrow
■ sock/pluck
■ wake/back

These introduce a feeling of uncertainty, perhaps suggesting that, despite the father's power, there will come a time when things will change.

Folio Reading Task

Show how Heaney establishes for us the relationship between himself and his father and then makes us think about relationships in general.

Seamus Heaney

27

Referring to more than one text

In your Standard Grade folio, you are not required to compare different texts in your Reading pieces. It is a very good learning experience, however, and is a skill you will have to show later – at Higher Grade, for example. You can develop this skill by following the advice and activities in this section. It is also helpful in writing about a text to be able to refer to another text by the same author.

There is more practical advice on writing about literature in a later section of the book (see page 50). It deals with what you should be writing in your Reading pieces, and also what possibilities there are in the folio.

 Make a list of any features which you think are typical of Heaney's poetry. These may be to do with content or style.

 Re-read "Storm on the Island" on pages 91.

REMEMBER As you are studying the poems of a particular poet, it will help you to note down what you think are the most typical features.

Try to find ways in which this poem is similar to, or different from, those you have already read. Look out for the following:

Alliteration

There are many examples of **alliteration** in "Storm on the Island". This technique is used to emphasize the sturdiness of the houses:

> we build our houses squat,
> Sink walls in rock and roof them with good slate.

The strength of Heaney's father in "Follower" was depicted in a similar fashion:

> His shoulders globed like a full sail strung.

Similar sounds

Heaney uses harsh consonants to give a cutting edge, as you have already found in "Digging":

> a clean rasping sound
> When the spade sinks into the gravelly ground.

This is also present in "Storm on the Island".

 Find as many examples of harsh consonants as you can in "Storm on the Island".

Conversational language

Another feature of Heaney's style is his use of conversational language. He keeps your feet firmly on the ground with his **colloquialisms**:

Sure isn't it better for them now? ("The Early Purges")

By God, the old man could handle a spade. ("Digging")

In "Storm on the Island", there are further examples:

- as you can see
- you know what I mean
- we just sit tight

Simple statements

Heaney often states things quite simply. Look at the following opening lines:

I sat all morning in the college sick bay ("Mid-Term Break")

I was six when I first saw kittens drown ("The Early Purges")

In a similar way, "Storm on the Island" opens quite ordinarily:

We are prepared.

 REMEMBER Underline similar styles of language in your texts and quote these when you write about them in your folio.

Effective descriptions

Heaney conveys powerful images through his use of language:

Like wet gloves they bobbed and shone ("The Early Purges")

The cold smell of potato mould, the squelch and slap
Of soggy peat ("Digging")

His shoulders globed like a full sail strung ("Follower")

(?) *In what ways is the storm described in "Storm on the Island"? How effective is this description?*

Seamus Heaney

Understatement

In "Storm on the Island", the gale is battering the houses but the poet reduces the force of the attack. He states that they were bombarded "by the empty air". His conclusion reduces the threat to a "huge nothing".

This use of understatement is typical of many of Heaney's final lines, like:

A four foot box, a foot for every year ("Mid-Term Break")

The final line forces the reader to think. In "Mid-Term Break", the abrupt ending raises questions about the poet's feelings towards his brother. "Storm on the Island" ends with "it is a huge nothing we fear". Most of the poem is taken up with the picture of a storm, but this fear is reduced to a "nothing". Why? What kind of a storm is this? Is the poem really about our fears? Are they really as terrifying as the storm seems to be? Or are they, like the "empty air", nothing to worry about?

The conclusions, like the poems themselves, are thought-provoking.

 REMEMBER Notice how many of Heaney's poems end with an understatement.

Photo: George Sutherland

Liz Lochhead

In order to understand Liz Lochhead's poetry, it helps to know some key facts about the writer:

- she was born in 1947
- she was brought up in Motherwell, Lanarkshire
- she went to Glasgow School of Art
- she taught Art for eight years before becoming a full-time writer
- she lives in Glasgow
- she travels in Britain and abroad giving performances of her work
- she writes poetry, drama and performance pieces
- she is one of the most successful and popular of Scottish writers.

Some features of Liz Lochhead's work which are dealt with in this book are:

- visual imagery
- identity
- voices
- sound
- language

 REMEMBER
Be aware of how a poet's writing has been influenced by events in his or her life.

Approaching her poems

You will find that Liz Lochhead is a very accessible writer; her poems can usually be enjoyed straight away, especially if they are read out loud. There is also a lot of humour in her work. However, you will find, when you look more closely at her poems, that they are very carefully constructed and have many layers of meaning. The poet uses language skilfully to create characters and make you think about ideas and feelings. She can take everyday situations and "make the ordinary extraordinary".

Liz Lochhead is a writer whose work is both strongly visual, and at the same time, playful with words, perhaps reflecting her interests in art and drama. She has said that her first attempts at writing tended to be "pictures in words", but to appreciate her work fully you need to hear it read aloud to take in the voice, tone and rhythm.

How to use this section

Three poems are examined in this section. "The Choosing" is examined in detail – it is used to explain how to approach a poem in order to find the meaning and select the key ideas. The other two poems, "Kidspoem/ Bairnsang" and "Box Room", are examined in order to highlight specific features. The "Kidspoem/Bairnsang" pages examine features of language, including issues related to Scots language, while the "Box Room" pages deal with voice and tone.

This section helps you in studying poetry, particularly in identifying a poem's overall meaning. This is very important when you are writing a critical evaluation based on a poem for your folio.

REMEMBER
"Kidspoem/ Bairnsang" and "Box Room" are not dealt with in as much detail as "The Choosing". Find the meaning and select key ideas yourself, using the section on "The Choosing" to help you.

"The Choosing" by Liz Lochhead

To find the meaning

- Read the poem through carefully, several times.
- Brainstorm it, jotting down your ideas about what you think it means.
- Select the key ideas.
- Find evidence in the poem to support these ideas.
- Jot down ideas of your own which might explain what the poem is about.

Read it through

When you come to read any poem, you must read it through at least once and, ideally, several times. Try to find answers to the following questions:

- Who is the poem about? Who is/are the main character/s?
- Where is the poem set? When does the "action" take place?
- What actually happens in the poem? What are its "events"?
- Who is "speaking" in the poem?
- Why has the poet chosen a particular title?

Now you should be ready to move on to more important questions.

REMEMBER Try to do some background reading. The examiner will reward the results of your research.

Brainstorm the poem

Here are some ideas that readers of "The Choosing" have come up with before, presented as a **brainstorm**. You will find the poem on page 91.

REMEMBER It usually helps to brainstorm a poem and look for all possible meanings.

education?
envy?
equality?
pressures?
making choices?
social class?

The Choosing

intelligence?
choices made for you?
achieving?
superiority?
university?
opportunity?
high school?
family and parents?
friendship?
career versus family?

Liz Lochhead

Select key ideas

◎ *Underline the points in the brainstorm list on page 31 which best match your ideas about "The Choosing". Add any other ideas you have about the poem.*

Find the evidence

◎ *Read the poem again and look for words, phrases or lines that reflect or support the points you have underlined.*

For example, you might agree that the poem has something to do with "equality". The evidence to support this could come from the first verse:

> We were first equal Mary and I

or from the second verse:

> common bond in being cleverest (equal)

You need to concentrate on deciding what the poet seems to be saying about "equality" or people being "equal". What kind of equality is she writing about? In what sense is she looking at it?

(?) *Are there further examples you could identify?*

Right or wrong?

The essay you write for your folio will be "right" or "successful" in the degree to which you offer ideas which are logically supported by evidence from the poem. Use the text itself as a solid foundation for your comments.

Practice Tasks

1 For each of the following ideas, write down a quotation from "The Choosing" to support the idea that the poem is saying something about it:

- envy
- people making choices
- education is not necessarily as important as some people believe
- social class
- choices are made for us by others

- achieving or achievement
- school is seen as important or unimportant
- opportunity is not available to everyone
- family and career are not easy to balance
- friendship

2 Select one of the other Liz Lochhead poems in the book. Brainstorm the poem. Match ideas with evidence from the poem.

📺 Use of language

The purpose of this section is to give you some help in the study of poetry, particularly in the area of identifying a poem's use of language. This is very important when you are writing a critical evaluation of a poem for your folio.

"The Choosing" by Liz Lochhead is looked at again in this section.

Imagery

Imagery is the use of figures of speech to create certain kinds of pictures for the reader.

 Look at the following lines from "The Choosing":

> Her arms are round the full-shaped vase
> that is her body

- What picture does the poet create for the reader here?

- How does she create this image or picture (try to pick out the key word in the lines)?

- What is the effect of the image?

There are several possibilities here. The poet, in using the image of the vase, suggests that Mary is expecting a baby. There is the idea that her body is a vessel, carrying something full of life. What other connotations (i.e. suggestions, implications, associations) are possible when you look at this image?

❓ *Are there any other examples of imagery in the poem (the use of figures of speech such as metaphor, simile etc.)? Quote them and write down your ideas about what they mean.*

REMEMBER
Always be alert to the different things with which a word can be associated.

REMEMBER
Always be on the look-out for different meanings and other possible interpretations.

Repetition

Poets commonly use repetition to help emphasise ideas and reinforce key points in a poem. In the first verse, Liz Lochhead uses repetition to some effect. This can be seen by the underlining of the key words:

> We were first <u>equal</u> Mary and I
> with the same coloured ribbons in mouse-coloured hair
> and with <u>equal</u> shyness,
> we curtseyed to the lady councillor
> for copies of Collins' Children's Classics.
> First <u>equal</u>, <u>equally</u> proud.

REMEMBER
Don't be too precise in saying that one word definitely means one thing only.

Liz Lochhead

A major idea in the first verse is that equality is something which the poet wants to say something about. She wants to make it clear that she and Mary were very close, so close that they were similar in everything. They were inseparable. Even the use of the word 'same' in this verse, and later in the poem, helps to re-inforce this emphasis.

Another question however, might be to ask if this emphasis is reflected throughout the poem. How far is this idea pursued? If it is not followed through the whole poem, where does it stop? If it stops, why has the poet not followed it through?

Sentence structure

◎ *In a few places in the poem, Liz Lochhead uses a distinctive sentence structure. Look at the following examples. What can you say about them?*

- First equal, equally proud *(verse 1)*
- same houses, different homes *(verse 3)*

REMEMBER Feel the rhythm of a poem by reading it aloud.

The first thing to notice might be the apparent balance of these two examples, how the phrasing seems to be equally weighted (try speaking or reciting these examples aloud; you will begin to feel the balance in the way they are written, the sense of the two phrases "mirroring" each other). They are also almost exactly the same length.

What about meaning and purpose? In the first example, you can see that this structure, due to its "balance" and "equalness", reflects the poet's point that she and Mary are equals in certain ways, that they are closely connected to each other.

In the second example, the same "balance" seems evident, but if you look closely at the words you can see a difference is also being suggested by the poet. What is this difference? This point seems to mark a turning point in the poem. In what way?

REMEMBER Find the basic pattern but notice the exceptions — these are important.

⑦ *Can you find other examples of sentences which appear to be "balanced", or pairs of sentences which reflect some sense of "balance", therefore indicating the poet's concern with the equality shared between Mary and herself? (You might, for example, study the early part of each of the first two verses.)*

Word choice

Finally, look at how the poet is careful about her word choice, but not in a figurative sense, as discussed earlier.

(?) *Why do you think Liz Lochhead chose to use the following words in the poem ?*

■ mouse (-coloured hair) *(verse 1)*

Did she want to suggest that she and Mary were timid and uncertain about themselves? Does she echo this by the choice of any other words in the first verse? What reasons might she have for describing the girls in this way?

■ glimpse *(verse 4)*

After she and Mary had gone their separate ways ("they moved", beginning of verse 4), she sees Mary's father, from a distance, briefly. What is she "glimpsing"? Is it Mary's father or is she briefly recalling their earlier closeness? Does this word suggest, in itself, that they have grown apart, where their contact, if any, is brief?

■ elegant (greyhounds) *(verse 4)*

(?) *What is the poet saying about Mary's father? Does he lack "class", "style", "breeding"?*

Practice Task

Re-read "The Choosing" on page 91.

Consider the following questions and try to write down ideas which answer them:

1 What does the poet suggest when Mary's father is described as

   mufflered *(verse 4)*?

2 What does the poet want to suggest by the description:

   ...our small school's small class *(verse 2)*?

3 Can you explain the associations the poet wants the reader to think about when she mentions "the housing scheme"?

4 Comment on the idea(s) contained in the statement that Mary's father "didn't believe in high school education" *(verse 4)*.

5 Is there anything significant in the statement which follows:

   especially for girls? *(verse 4)*

6 What kind of attitude do you think is revealed when Liz Lochhead says:

   Oh, you can see where the attraction lies in Mary's life *(verse 5)*?

7 Would it make any difference to the meaning if the poet had not written "really" at the end of the last line in verse 5?

8 Try to explain what it means when it says:

I think of those prizes that were ours for the taking *(verse 6)*

9 What does it mean when it says:

(I) ...wonder when the choices got made we don't remember making *(verse 6)*?

Liz Lochhead

"Kidspoem/Bairnsang" by Liz Lochhead

At first sight this poem may seem to be an account of a wee girl's first day at school. Yet when we look at it closely, we can see that it deals with language and identity, and explores the connection between who we are and the way we speak and write. You will find the poem on page 91.

The story

The narrator (the person telling the story) of the poem describes the weather, what she is wearing and what her mother says as she goes to school. The story is repeated three times:

- in the Scots voice of the child and her mother
- in the English voice she learns at school
- in the Scots voice she says she learns "to forget" at school.

Looking at language

Scots/English

Look at the Scots and English versions of the girl's first day at school.

There are many pairs of words or phrases which are equivalent – for example:

> *gey dreich*   *really dismal*

They may mean roughly the same but the effect of the Scots word and the English word is often different. Say each word out loud and listen to the sounds. For example, "dismal" has a dull, depressing sound but "dreich" suggests the sound of rain and wind, giving a it more physical quality. "Gey" sounds harsher than "really", emphasizing how bad the weather was.

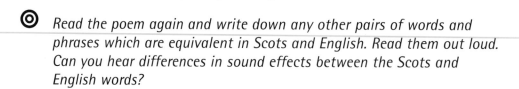

Read the poem again and write down any other pairs of words and phrases which are equivalent in Scots and English. Read them out loud. Can you hear differences in sound effects between the Scots and English words?

Private/public

As well as pairs of words which are Scots/English, you can also find words which show that the first section of the poem is in the girl's home language while the English section of the poem is the language of school; a public, rather than private place – for example:

> *mum*   *mother*   *bum*   *bottom*

The first words in these pairs are colloquial words which tend to be used in informal situations between people who know each other very well.

(?) *Do you think the poem suggests that Scots is regarded as a language which can only be used for family matters and is not suited to the outside world?*

Spoken/written

Not only does the narrator learn to speak a different language (English/public) at school, she also learns to forget the private Scots language of home. There is no way to write it so it remains a spoken language with less status than English. The last stanza explores the differences between the spoken and written word. Because you learned to write in English and had to read it out in a certain way you sounded as if:

> you were grown up, posh, male, English and dead.

These are all the opposite of the girl, who is not any of these things. The written language she learns in school does not reflect who she is.

(?) *What do you think the tone of the last stanza is (if you are not sure about what tone is, look at the section about tone on page 38)?*

(?) *Is the girl angry, amused, disgusted, confused? What are her feelings and attitudes about the way she is expected to write and speak in school?*

! **R E M E M B E R** Read poems aloud and feel the tone that the poet is using. Listen to recordings of the poems.

! **R E M E M B E R** Always be ready for the shifts in tone which indicate a change of mood. You will receive extra credit if you can recognise them.

Structure

All poems have a shape. This poem is called "Kidspoem/Bairnsang" and the way it is shaped or structured reflects the idea of a children's rhyme, though it does not have a regular rhyme scheme. Repetition is used a lot (though the words differ in the Scots and English versions of the child's story).

> It was January
> and a gey dreich day
>
> It was January
> and a really dismal day
>
> the first day I went to (the) school.

The poem seems to be written in a kind of circle until the final stanza, with the Scots, then English, then Scots versions of the story following each other around.

Linking words are used and are placed on a line by themselves: so, said, so, said, so. Then the final section is introduced by 'Oh'. Look at the punctuation of the poem. Up until the last stanza, there are no full stops. What effect does this create? Why do you think the poet has chosen to write in this way?

Summing up

(?) *Do you think there is a message in this poem? What do you think the narrator is saying about the way in which she was educated?*

Liz Lochhead

"Box Room" by Liz Lochhead

Voice

A writer creates poems or stories by choosing combinations of words to capture events, ideas and feelings. In reading and responding to poetry, it is important to consider not just what is said but also whose voice or voices you are hearing. Unless you can hear the voice in the poem and find the person to whom it belongs believable, the poem will not work for you.

Several of Liz Lochhead's poems include the voices of more than one character – rather like a little drama. "Box Room" is an example of this. With writers like Liz Lochhead, it can seem that their poems are reporting actual people and events from their own lives, or that it is the writer's own voice speaking. Although the writer draws on her experience, the poem is made up, just as a play is. You will find the poem on page 92.

Tone

❗ REMEMBER Using the voice of more than one character in a poem can help to create contrasting tones.

The way in which things are said is as important as what is said; this is what is meant by tone. It's similar to when you listen to someone talk and you can tell whether they are happy, angry, sad or pleased from the sound of their voice as well as the words they use.

In a written poem, the writer cannot rely upon actual sound. So as well as the choice of words, the way the poet arranges the lines on the page and uses punctuation can help you to work out how the voice or voices should sound.

◎ *Read the poem several times. Read it out loud – this can be the best way to begin to understand the poem and to hear what it is telling us.*

The poem tells the story of a girl's first visit to her boyfriend's mother's house. She has come to stay, to establish herself as a permanent fixture, but she has not anticipated the welcome she actually encounters or the effect this visit will have on her feelings about her relationship with the boy.

 What is the tone of this poem? Is it the same throughout? How has it been created?

Look at the opening lines. The girl at first tries to be assertive, apparently confident that the mother is to be pitied for keeping the boy's room as a

> pathetic
> Shrine to your lost boyhood

But there are immediate signs of uneasiness and an awkward atmosphere.

The poem opens with three short sentences, the third one broken up by a line ending. How do they sound when you read them? You have to break them up, creating a choppy, irregular rhythm. The poem as a whole has a regular structure of pairs of rhyming lines, or **rhyming couplets**, which usually give a more flowing, calm effect. The effect here suggests uncertainty, despite "smiles all round".

Almost as soon as she is through the door, her boyfriend's mother "put me in my place" – the dash used here also forces you to pause and break up the flow. You hear the girl's thoughts as she listens to the mother, and later, as she looks more closely at her surroundings. Some of these comments are in brackets, or parentheses, which also break the flow.

(?) *What else might the brackets suggest? Might they give the reader the sense of being drawn into the story, of seeing it from the girl's point of view?*

The attitude of the mother is captured very clearly in what she said to the girl, and in the tone she used.

(?) *What kind of tone do you think she might have used when she spoke of him giving up his childhood bed for "a Friend"? Why do you suppose that the word "friend" has a capital letter here?*

Is the mother letting the girl know that her connection to her son is only temporary? Can the capital letter give the word a different effect, so that although she says "friend" she is suggesting "stranger"?

(?) *The mother's tone is one of frosty politeness. How does her language establish her own permanent place in her son's affections?*

The mother speaks of what "always" happens, of her son's returning "home", she speaks of him "making do" which is "All right/for a night or two". He's only slept there "Once or twice before". In other words, the girl is part of occasional, purely temporary arrangements which disrupt their happy home, but which are tolerated out of politeness towards a guest – a guest is, by definition, only temporary.

As the poem progresses and the girl is left to contemplate her boyfriend's childhood "shrine", her initial confidence in their relationship wavers. The tone of the second stanza of the poem is hesitant, questioning and then fearful. Not even the electric blanket can stop the girl's shivers.

As you read on through the poem, you will see that the tone is conveyed in all of the ways mentioned: rhythm, use of language and punctuation.

 Read through the second stanza. Explain how the writer manages to convey the girl's growing uncertainty and fear. Include comments on the rhythm, use of language and punctuation.

Practice Task

Look at the other two Liz Lochhead poems in this section. Choose one and write about the tone of the poem, noting any changes or shifts. In addition to use of language, rhythm and punctuation, you might consider the effect of using repetition.

"Peace" by Rupert Brooke

The poets who wrote at the time of the First World War were affected by it in different ways. In the beginning, before they experienced the horrors of trench warfare, some poets wrote about the wonderful opportunities war offered young men.

(?) *What do you think you might feel if your country became involved in a war – fear, anger, excitement?*

◎ *Read "Peace" by Rupert Brooke on page 92.*

Meaning

As you can see, the poem's title is ironic: it is not about peace. Brooke welcomes the chance to go to war and thanks God for it. He believes that war has given young people something to do:

> and wakened us from sleeping

He thinks that they live in "a world grown old and cold and weary" and that people were not achieving the most they could. They were "half-men". War would do this country good.

◎ *List words and phrases that show how Brooke feels about his country. Explain what difference he thinks war will make.*

Language

Brooke conveys his attitude to war not only by what he says, but by:

- the words he uses
- the ways he puts words together.

He sees war as a God-given opportunity. The first four lines sound triumphant, celebrating this opportunity. The young have been "wakened". Up until now, their lives have been spent simply "sleeping". Brooke sees the chance to fight as a chance for young men to cleanse themselves. War will be a kind of purification:

> To turn, as swimmers into cleanness leaping

The word "leaping" suggests that men will go to war with energy and enthusiasm. The line also marks a change in the poem as the focus shifts to peacetime in this country. All the images now are negative ones:

- a world grown old
- sick hearts
- half-men
- dirty songs and dreary

Honour, he says, cannot move these men. He even shows love as a small and empty experience.

 Look at the list you have already made and the phrases listed on the previous page. Explain how they present a depressed picture of peacetime society. Now compare them to these phrases from the first five lines of the poem:

- caught our youth
- clear eye
- wakened us from sleeping
- sharpened power
- hand made sure
- into cleanness leaping

Tone

The poem sounds like a kind of prayer. It begins with words of praise to the Lord:

> Now God be thanked Who has
> matched us with His hour

The word "and" is repeated seven times in the poem. This creates a sense of continuity and lets the poet link each idea closely to the one before and the one after it.

The rhymes also tie the ideas together. Sometimes the effect is one of contrast:

"wakened us from sleeping" and "into cleanness leaping".

At other times, Brooke uses the rhyme to stress the decay in society:

"cold and weary" and "dirty songs and dreary".

The poet pairs words to reinforce the ideas:

"a world grown old" is also "cold and weary";

the "hand made sure" is accompanied by a "clear eye".

Brooke is perhaps so enthusiastic in his celebration of war because he wants to encourage his readers to volunteer for service. The poem captures the national mood of optimism which existed when it was written. Many people believed that war would be a good thing and, after all, it would be over in six weeks and the men would be home for Christmas.

REMEMBER Always be aware of how the War Poets used religious ideas and words.

Folio Reading Task

Show how Brooke organises his ideas and uses language to persuade his reader that the announcement of war is a thing to be celebrated.

(You should underline the key words in this task and shape your writing piece to deal with the ideas they emphasise.)

"The Soldier" by Rupert Brooke

◎ *Read "The Soldier" by Rupert Brooke on page 92.*

Meaning

This poem was written as Brooke prepared to leave to fight at Gallipoli in Turkey. In it, he foresees his death in a foreign country. He believes that when he dies and his body turns to dust, it will be a better, "richer" dust than the earth in which it will be buried. The reason is that his dust will have been made by all the good things which are to be found in his own country, England:

> A body of England's breathing English air,
> Washed by the rivers, blest by suns of home.

For him, this is not a matter for sadness. In death, his body will give back those values learned in England, the values which he feels are so important:

> Laughter, learnt of friends; and gentleness,
> In hearts at peace, under an English heaven.

Brooke uses the word "England" repeatedly throughout the poem. It represents not only a country or a place, but a set of values. We all come from dust, the poet is saying, but he has the advantage of being shaped by English dust. Is it patriotic, or nationalistic?

⑦ *How does Brooke present England as a kind of paradise? Compare this view of England with the view of the unnamed society he presented in "Peace".*

Form

 REMEMBER You don't have to explain the technical details of what a sonnet is in your Reading piece, but you should make clear that you understand how a poet uses the sonnet.

Brooke has chosen to write his poem as a **sonnet**, a form commonly used by poets when they want to express personal feelings. This sonnet is divided into two stanzas. The first contains eight lines (an octet) and the second contains six lines (a sestet). Each has its own rhyme scheme. In the first stanza, it is AB AB CD CD. In the second, it is EFG EFG. The rhyme schemes separate the stanzas, but they also bind the ideas together in each stanza.

First stanza

The first stanza is concerned with the possibility that the poet may be killed abroad and his body buried in a foreign country.

Second stanza

The subject of the poem turns on the word "and" at the beginning of the second stanza. Here, Brooke considers what his death can give back to England or to the next generation.

Here are some possible reasons why Brooke chose the sonnet form:

■ it is a classical and regular form, like the verse that might be found on a gravestone

■ it has always been associated with expressing personal ideas

■ the two stanzas help the poet to deal with separate, but related ideas.

(?) *Explain how Brooke uses the two-stanza form of the sonnet to look at separate, though related, ideas.*

Tone

The overall tone of "The Soldier" is one of personal reflection. A religious feel is given by the rather formal movement of the verse. Brooke uses phrases connected with religious ceremony:

■ think only this

■ that is forever

■ there shall be

The balanced phrases within the line make it seem formal:

"A body of England's" is balanced by "breathing English air".

"Washed by the rivers" has its counterpart "blest by suns of home".

The poet gives an air of formality to lines by first stating an idea and then developing it:

"A dust whom England bore" goes on to be "shaped, made aware".

There is a sense of lightness and calm created through the focus on happy memories:

"Her sights and sounds", "Dreams happy as her day", "And, laughter, learnt of friends"

These features combine to give the feeling of a man contemplating his coming death. There is sadness since his body will be turned to dust, but also a quiet feeling of optimism, that his death will have some purpose. The values he has learnt will be given back. He will not have died in vain. Ironically, Rupert Brooke himself died of illness before his troopship reached Gallipoli and he was buried in "a foreign field".

Folio Reading Task

1 How effectively does Brooke convey his view in this poem? What are your thoughts and feelings about this?

2 What effect do you think it would have on someone whose loved one was at war?

World War I poetry

📺 "Attack" by Siegfried Sassoon

Poets who fought at the front were faced with the harsh realities of war. Their writing reflected their experiences. The patriotic feelings of Brooke's poetry were soon replaced by quite different emotions brought out by the mud and slaughter of the trenches.

◎ *Read "Attack" by Siegfried Sassoon on page 93.*

Meaning

There is a clear difference between Sassoon's experience and that of Brooke. The difference is reflected in what he writes about. Sassoon wanted people to know what was going on. In "Attack", he writes about an actual dawn raid. He describes the men going over the top into battle.

His poem is concerned with the pointlessness of war. He writes, not of heroism or idealism, but of the reality of trench warfare:

> tanks creep and topple forward to the wire

He writes from actual experience. He describes precisely the way tanks moved on the battlefield. The gunfire is real:

> The barrage roars and lifts

He captures the moment of men floundering in mud. He states what happens, as a war reporter might:

> They leave their trenches, going over the top

He ends with a desperate plea for this kind of slaughter to stop.

❓ *What do you think the people at home would have learned about trench warfare from reading this poem?*

Language

❗ REMEMBER Concentrate in your writing on how the poet presents his experience of war.

The poem is made up of three long sentences broken up by the short statement, "The barrage roars and lifts". It is as though Sassoon is piling one detail on top of the other, reflecting the grim inevitability of the whole process. The abrupt exclamation at the end is a sign of desperation and an attempt to involve the reader in that feeling.

There are strong images throughout the poem. The "glow'ring sun" is portrayed as:

> Smouldering through spouts of drifting smoke that shroud
> The menacing scarred slope

❓ *Think about the effects of the words "glow'ring", "smouldering", "drifting", "shroud", "menacing", and "scarred" as they appear in this image. How do they create a sense of danger and death? Write down your ideas.*

Personification

In the previous example, the slope is described as "menacing". It is given a human characteristic to suggest it is both threatening and dangerous. This form of **imagery** is known as **personification** – the object becomes like a person. Sassoon uses personification often in this poem.

 Think about these images:

- *time ticks blank and busy on their wrists*

- *hope, with furtive eyes and grappling fists,
  flounders in mud*

  *Explain how Sassoon has personified time and hope.
  Do you think these images are effective?*

Tone

There is a sense of distancing in this poem. The whole scene is shrouded in mist and the soldiers are not shown as individuals, but as an indistinct group with their faces hidden:

Lines of grey, muttering faces, masked with fear

Although Sassoon describes in detail what is happening, there is a sense of unreality to the scene – almost like a dream or nightmare.

The poem moves relentlessly on, almost as if the writer is in a trance. The sun rises and the tanks move forward as the men leave their trenches. As they flounder in the mud, the poet can bear it no longer and he cries out:

Jesus, make it stop!

This is the cry of a real man in a real situation. The colloquial outburst, breaking into the trance-like atmosphere, pulls the reader back to reality. It is as if the poet is waking from a nightmare. He hopes his cry will be heard back home.

Folio Reading Task

How does Sassoon use language effectively to convey his ideas to the reader?

World War I poetry

BITESIZEenglish

"Dulce et Decorum est" by Wilfred Owen

Like Sassoon, Owen was appalled by what was going on in the war. He intensified the attack on those responsible for the fighting and tried to undermine the belief that war was glorious.

◎ *Read "Dulce et Decorum est" by Wilfred Owen on page 93.*

Meaning

❗ R E M E M B E R
Always be aware of the mixture of reality and unreality in the work of the War Poets.

As Sassoon does in "Attack", Owen mixes reality and unreality to get his message across. But in Owen's poetry, the sense of reality is more vivid. He describes a scene of war, made more vivid by his own involvement:

we cursed through sludge

He draws the reader into the poem by comparing his situation to a more familiar one, "like old beggars under sacks". He takes the reader along with them on their march, saying: "Men marched asleep" and "All went lame; all blind." He recreates the start of a gas attack:

Gas! GAS! Quick boys!

He shows that the man has to shout "Gas" louder a second time, because the men are too tired to hear.

Next, there is a bitter description of the man who doesn't put on his gas mask in time. The image of the man helplessly "drowning" in the gas is one that haunts his sleep and one which he feels he has to share with his reader:

If you could hear...

Owen's anger at this waste of life is shown in his description of the man's suffering, "obscene as cancer".

◎ *Imagine you're a soldier in Owen's regiment who witnessed this scene. Describe, in your own words, what you experienced and saw.*
This is not a folio task. However, it is valuable learning practice.

Language

The poem falls into four stages:

■ the men marching
■ the gas attack in which the man fails to put on his gas mask
■ the events following this
■ the appeal to the reader.

◎ *Make a list of the images used to describe the men in the first eight lines of the poem. Think about the meaning of each image separately. Put together, what kind of picture do they create?*

Now look at lines 9–16. When the attack comes, the fumbling for a gas mask is described as "ecstasy" – the most heightened of sensations. The soldier who doesn't fit his in time is like "a man in fire or lime". The poem becomes dream-like as Owen sees him dimly through his own mask. The scene is like being "under a green sea" and the man is "drowning".

In the final stanza, the ugly and bitter images create a sense of wickedness and evil. The man is flung into the wagon, his eyes "writhing" and his face a "devil's sick of sin". The adjectives "froth-corrupted", "obscene", "bitter", "vile" and "incurable" follow one after another, leaving the reader in no doubt of the horror of the scene.

Suddenly, the horror stops. The reader is addressed as "My friend" and finally Owen speaks out about the "old lie" which England has been suffering from. He expresses it in Latin:

> Dulce et decorum est
> Pro patria mori

This means "it is sweet and noble to die for one's country". Would the people who preach about war say the same thing if they had seen what Owen had seen?

Latin was an important subject in the education system of Owen's day. The poet knew that it would be very familiar to his readers. They would have studied the poems of Horace, the author of these lines, at school and would see the **irony** that was contained in Owen's version, that it was sweet and noble to die for one's native country.

Tone

The tone is bitter and sarcastic. The poet's anger is felt in the cutting **alliteration**: "Bent double like old beggars".

The harsh consonants convey his feelings:

> Come gargling from the froth-corrupted lungs

Mixed in with the harsh reality are the dream-like passages in which Owen softens the tone:

> Dim through the misty panes and thick green light

Here, the gentle consonants and softer sounds of the words give a muffled effect. This shifting from the harsh reality of battle to a trance-like state, and back again, is very effective. Owen is suggesting the state of mind of the exhausted troops. They are engaged in a real fight, but it all seems unreal.

Folio Reading Task

How does Owen try in "Dulce et Decorum est" to convince the reader that war is evil?

You should refer to his use of ideas, language and tone.

"Strange Meeting" by Wilfred Owen

In "Dulce et Decorum est", Owen starts in the middle of the fighting. In "Strange Meeting", he begins by escaping from the battlefield. This poem was not published while he was alive. Strangely, it was found among his papers after he was killed in 1918, just before the war ended.

Meaning

 Read through the poem carefully – preferably aloud – making sure you understand its meaning. You will find it on page 93.

Owen imagines that one of the tunnels, in which soldiers took cover from shellfire, led deeper to where a group of sleeping men was to be found. He can't decide whether they are asleep or dead.

When he prods one of the figures, the man jumps up and Owen realises from his gestures that they are both in hell. The poet is surprised that no blood seeped down from the trenches and that there was no sound of gunfire as there would have been in a frontline tunnel.

This "strange friend" reveals what the war has meant for him – wasted years, the loss of true beauty, and, much worse, the truth which has been suppressed:

> The pity of war, the pity war distilled

The friend goes on to say that future generations will have to put up with what they have ruined. He would like to bring back lost innocence:

> I would go up and wash them from sweet wells

He would have made every effort:

> I would have poured my spirit without stint

He wanted to save the world, but not through war, which he calls a "cess" (an open sewer). He then confesses that he is the enemy the poet killed. He recognises Owen because he is wearing the same expression that he wore when he killed him:

> for so you frowned
> Yesterday through me as you jabbed and killed.

He concludes by suggesting that they should "sleep now".

Language

Owen creates a vision of hell, but it is a hell which grows out of the battlefield, the soldier's own hell: "dull tunnel", "guns thumped, or down the flues made moan".

The well-known places and events of war are exaggerated in the poem. The tunnels have been "scooped through granites". The war is described as a struggle between the gods ("Titanic wars"). The poem refers to more ancient wars, "when much blood had clogged their chariot wheels", as though the Great War encompasses all wars.

In his regret for his lost youth, the strange friend speaks of lost ideals of hope and beauty. He talks of lost opportunities for laughter:

For by my glee might many men have laughed.

Tone

The overall tone is one of regret. Owen is sickened by the waste and loss, but he does not sound angry. Everything happens in a dream-like atmosphere. The whole poem is a sort of vision in which one man meets in hell the man he killed the day before. The poem ends with the peaceful "Let us sleep now".

Cross-referencing

Brooke was keen to go to war. He joined up as soon as war was declared, but died soon afterwards. Owen served in the trenches, where he suffered shell-shock. He was awarded the Military Cross. The two men's different experiences of war are clearly reflected in their poetry.

Differences and similarities

In "The Soldier", Brooke writes of the "laughter learnt of friends" as something important. In "Strange Meeting", Owen writes that one of the soldiers regrets that "by my glee might many men have laughed". Both poets value laughter in life.

◎ *List the main differences between the poetry of Brooke and Owen.*

Brooke's poems are full of youthful enthusiasm and patriotic ideas. The pathos in Owen's poems lies in the fact that all these ideas have been wasted. Think about the attitudes of both the poets to war and how these attitudes are conveyed through their poems.

Like Brooke, Owen uses words such as "old", "weary", "sick", "dirty", "dreary". Notice the difference in effect. Owen uses them to write about the horrors of war – his dirt and dreariness belong to the filth of the trenches, not the country he left behind.

Can you find other similarities in the language and writing technique of the two poets?

Folio Reading Task

Compare "Strange Meeting" and "Dulce et Decorum est". You should consider:

■ what the poems are about

■ the attitudes to war

■ the use of realism and fantasy

■ how the main ideas are presented.

Writing about literature

You will be expected to show Reading and Writing skills in the folio and the exams. The teaching and learning of these skills is based on:

■ reading texts, both fiction and non-fiction
■ writing about them
■ producing pieces of writing like them.

Read the following points very carefully as they can be confusing otherwise.

■ Writing skills are required in both the Folio Writing and in the Writing examination.

■ Reading skills are required in both the Folio Reading and in the Reading examination.

■ Writing skills are the same in Folio and Examination.

■ Reading in the examination is what we usually think of as interpretation, or close reading. You provide short answers to questions on a passage or extract of prose.

■ Reading in the Folio, however, is about your response to imaginative literature – prose, poetry, drama or media texts.

■ You show your skills in this kind of Reading by writing about the literature you have read.

Your teacher will set you tasks or assignments for Folio Reading pieces. These tasks are designed to help you to show the SQA examiners that you can:

■ understand
■ analyse
■ appreciate the writer's craft in
■ show a personal stance to

any work of literature that you have studied.

The actual requirements that the examiners use for assessing your work are called the GRC (Grade Related Criteria) and your teacher can show you these on a checklist. They are also the targets that you aim for in writing your essay, so you should see them. The folio piece you produce will be a critical evaluation or imaginative response to literature (IRL). (Ask your teacher about this). There are certain key things you must bring into your writing about literature.

Purpose

You must pay close attention to the purpose of what you are doing. The task set by your teacher will make clear what you are to do. It is meant to help you to demonstrate your skills in Reading, as required by the GRC. When you understand the purpose of your writing, stick to it. It helps if you say at the beginning what you are setting out to do.

When writing your folio Reading pieces, you will have to present your material effectively. Follow these key steps:

- read the task carefully and make sure you understand it – if you don't, ask
- look for the key word or words that tell you what to do
- underline these words.

Suppose the task says, "By examining the language in The Early Purges, show how Heaney succeeds in communicating his ideas..."

There are at least two things to consider when responding to this task:

- the main emphasis of the task is on the <u>language</u>, not the content of the poem
- there is a question of <u>how successful</u> he is.

To decide how successful Heaney is, you must analyse the ways in which he uses language.

First, find examples of language use. Then make notes on their effect.

When you write the piece, use the formula: PQD.

- P stands for the POINT you want to make
- Q stands for QUOTATION
- D stands for DEVELOPMENT of the point.

If you use this formula, it will prevent you from repeating yourself, and you will be presenting your material effectively.

You could start, perhaps, with:
"The language chosen by Seamus Heaney in his poem, The Early Purges, is what contributes mainly to the success of the poem..."

You could then go on to deal with the words and phrases that the poet uses to show how he succeeds. For example:

"In this poem, Heaney uses the language of real people (POINT). Dan Taggart refers to the kittens as "the scraggy wee shits" (QUOTATION). By referring to the kittens in this way, Taggart seems to have no feeling for them. They are something to get rid of. On the other hand, he describes them as "wee", which suggests some kind of pity, a softening of feeling, as in the phrase "poor wee things". Perhaps Heaney wants to show Taggart as torn between his duty to rid the farm of unnecessary cats and his natural liking for them (DEVELOPMENT)."

This would be the start of a good Reading piece, because by using the PQD formula, you would advance the argument and show real understanding both of the poem and of the right way to carry out the task.

To make your purpose clear and show that you are aware of it, tell the reader directly what you intend to do, remind the reader that you are doing it, and finally that you have done it. This makes it clear that you know the purpose of your writing.

Knowledge

You have to deal with a whole text in your Reading piece, and the examiners expect to find that you really know about it. You should say very briefly what the poem (for example) is about. Use quotations and other references to the language of the poem to support the points you are making about how that language works.

In the unit on literary texts, you will have come across several important pieces of information. These concern the authors' lives, their times and what influenced their writing. Your folio pieces will not always need to include anything about the life of the author or the background. Sometimes biographical material will help, but it should never be extensive. The text (the author's work) is what matters most. For example, we know that the First World War poets were influenced by events, so some reference to them would be sensible if you were writing about "Dulce et Decorum Est". On the other hand, we know so little of the life of Shakespeare, that it is hardly ever necessary to refer to it in writing about *Macbeth*, for example. It might be appropriate for some tasks to refer to what people believed about witchcraft in his time. The new King, James VI, was very interested in it, and *Macbeth* was presented for the King.

Personal stance

The examiners really do want to know what you think about the literature. They know what the critics think already, and there is nothing that they can learn about what you think if your essay consists simply of other people's ideas regurgitated. Certain things are factual, of course, and cannot be changed, but in a poem of any substance, there is room for your interpretation and your personal views. Your view could be as valid as that of the actual writer, so don't be afraid to say what you think about the work, provided you can back up what you have to say with sensible comment. However, do not assert your view as if it were the only possible one.

The reason for studying literature is not so that you can quote poems off by heart, or have a detailed knowledge of the plot of the one novel you have read, or to pass an exam. It is so that you can learn to appreciate and set your own values on whatever creative works you might read or view throughout your life.

Attempt to write critical evaluations of the texts you have studied with BITESIZE. Before reading the points which follow each question, try to plan the writing piece for yourself. Always provide a suitable introduction and conclusion to your piece. Remember your audience and purpose.

Folio Reading Task 1 – Macbeth

Compare the relationship between Macbeth and Lady Macbeth in the Banquet Scene (Act 3, scene iv) with their relationship when they are planning to murder King Duncan (Act 1, scene vii).

- Introduction

In Act 3, scene iv: the Banquet Scene

- Lady Macbeth plays the concerned hostess who reminds Macbeth of his duties ("You do not give the cheer").

- She tries to excuse her husband's behaviour ("My lord is often thus/ And hath been from his youth").

- She tries to shake him out of his fear by taunting him about his vivid imagination ("This is the air-drawn dagger which, you said,/ Led you to Duncan").

- Macbeth tries to justify his behaviour ("If I stand here, I saw him")

- By persisting in her criticism, Lady Macbeth persuades Macbeth to confess his weakness ("I have a strange infirmity, which is nothing/To those who know me").

- Macbeth is amazed that his wife is unmoved by the ghost's presence ("When now I think you can behold such sights/ And keep the natural ruby of your cheeks").

- She feels the source of his troubles is lack of sleep ("you lack the season of all natures, sleep").

In Act 1, scene vii: planning the murder

- Lady Macbeth persuades her reluctant husband to murder Duncan. She taunts him (Macbeth: "We will proceed no further in the business"; Lady Macbeth: "Was the hope drunk wherein you dressed yourself?")

- She criticises his manhood ("When you durst do it, then you were a man").

- She tries to shock him into following her advice by using violent imagery ("I would while it was smiling in my face have pluck'd the nipple from his boneless gums,/ And dash'd the brains out").

- When Macbeth appears uncertain about their plan she encourages him

❗ REMEMBER Make sure you bring together points of similarity and difference.

("We fail!/ But screw your courage to the sticking-place").

■ She does the planning ("his two chamberlains/ Will I with wine and wassail so convince").

■ She tries to convince him that they are invincible ("What cannot you and I perform").

■ Macbeth is impressed by her ability ("Bring forth men-children only")

■ Macbeth is finally convinced and becomes interested in the details of the operation ("When we have mark'd with blood those sleepy two")

■ Finally, he decides to take his wife's advice about concealing his real intentions ("False face must hide what the false heart doth know")

■ Conclusion

Folio Reading Task 2 – Seamus Heaney

Explain what Seamus Heaney has to say in the poem "Digging" about the relationship between his skills and those of his father and grandfather, and how he uses language to convey his ideas effectively.

■ Introduction

■ The skills of Heaney and his father and grandfather, though different in many ways, do have some similarities.

■ The poet's tool is his pen ("The squat pen").

■ It is a powerful weapon ("snug as a gun").

■ His father works rhythmically as does the poet writing in verse ("Stooping in rhythm").

■ His father produced things of beauty ("Loving their cool hardness").

■ His father and grandfather were skilled in their trade ("By God, the old man could handle a spade").

■ His grandfather had a reputation for his ability ("My grandfather could cut more turf in a day...") whilst Heaney won the Nobel Prize for Literature.

■ Heaney decides to use his pen as a spade to dig with, to unearth ideas/poems/language ("I'll dig with it.")

Folio Reading Task 3 – Liz Lochhead

The appeal of Liz Lochhead's poems lies in her clever use of language. Choose one or more of the poems you have been studying to explain why you agree or disagree with this statement.

When you answer this question, try to discuss the poet's use of at least three of the following typical language features:

- visual imagery

- word choice

- rhyme

- rhythm

- dialect

- structure

Folio Reading Task 4 – World War I poetry

Consider both the message and the language that Rupert Brooke uses in his poem, "The Soldier". How well does the language support his message?

- Introduction

In "The Soldier", Brooke idealises England, thinking of it as a country:

- which brings up its men in the right way ("A dust whom England bore, shaped, made aware")

- which can make foreign countries into better places, even in death ("In that rich earth a richer dust concealed")

- whose influence is felt even after death ("Gives somewhere back the thoughts by England given")

- which allows peaceful values to flourish ("gentleness/ in hearts of peace, under an English heaven")

Brooke uses:

- the sonnet form to give the poem a classical dignity

- personification ("A dust whom England bore, shaped, made aware")

- images of paradise to idealise England ("dreams happy as her day")

- the regular rhyme scheme and rhythm which show the poet's confidence in his beliefs

- soft sounds to create an atmosphere of peace and contentment ("Her sights and sounds; dreams happy as her day")

- Conclusion

Reading skills

Standard Grade uses the word **Reading** to cover writing about literature as well as the kind of reading that we now call close reading or interpretation. In Standard Grade, you will show your close reading skills in the Reading examination.

The reading you find in the Reading paper and in the course could be either fiction or non-fiction. Though we have dealt separately with fiction in the unit on literary texts, much of what follows is still relevant to fiction and other works of literature, although it concentrates on non-fiction texts.

Non-fiction texts are written to inform, to persuade, to advise, to describe. As you already know, fiction texts have similar purposes.

What skills do I need? And where?

You are expected to be able to:

■ recognise the main concerns of the text
■ retrieve information from the text
■ draw **inferences** from the text
■ distinguish fact and opinion
■ comment on the writer's point of view
■ follow and explain the writer's **argument**
■ select material according to purpose
■ write about the author's technique
■ consider how effectively the writer conveys meaning.

This is not as difficult as it sounds.

How can I improve my reading skills?

To respond well to a text and do well in exams, you need to be an efficient reader. In a task or exam, the first thing to do is to read the **rubric** carefully. When you read the passage or extract and the questions, you will then have a very clear idea of your purpose in reading. In exam situations, it's very common for people to think that they've been given the wrong question paper, because it seems so hard!

 REMEMBER Underline key words and phrases in the text once you are sure of your purpose in reading that text.

You should also scan the questions. The second reading will be much better, and you will be looking for specific information you need for an answer. When you scan, you are using one set of information to inform your reading of another set of information. Every time someone asks you a question, they also provide you with a certain amount of information. In this kind of exercise, the questions tell you what to look for in your reading. So:

■ Read the rubric (what you've to do)   [Purpose]
■ Read the passage or text   [Main ideas]

- Read the questions   [Task]
- Read the passage again   [Scanning, locating, checking]

It helps if you always remember:

- whatever the text you are reading, it was written by a person

- someone had a particular purpose in writing it

- that person had a special reason for writing it in that way.

All of these things should come through in your reading.

◎ *Study these texts and work out why they were written, and for what kind of publication.*

How to Vote
A

This leaflet tells you how you can still vote even if you are unable to go to your polling station on election day. Providing there is a good reason why you cannot vote in person, you can apply to vote by post or proxy.
(A proxy is someone who votes on your behalf).

For example:
- if you will be away on holiday (in the UK or abroad);
- if your work takes you away from home;
- if you are ill or in hospital.

Some people qualify to vote by post or proxy for a longer period of time, not just at one particular election.

You will need to say on the application form whether you want to vote by post or by proxy.

If you want to vote by post you must give the full address to which your ballot paper should be sent. It must be in the United Kingdom. Postal ballot papers are normally sent out about a week before polling day.

If you want to appoint a proxy to vote for you, he or she must be:
- willing to vote on your behalf;
- a British citizen or citizen of the Commonwealth or the Republic of Ireland; or for local government and European Parliamentary elections, a citizen of the European Union;
- old enough to vote and legally allowed to vote.

Castle: A fortified defensive building.
B
Its name derives from the Latin word *castellum*, a small fortified place. The castle underwent many changes in its history to counteract the development of increasingly powerful weapons. In the early middle ages a castle consisted of a simple building on a mound of earth surrounded by a wooden fence (the motte and bailey castle), a design later copied in stone. The simplest stone castle, such as the White Tower of London, is called a keep or donjon. Later designs became more complicated, involving extensive outworks of battlemented towers and walls (curtain walls), e.g. Caernarfon Castle in Wales. As they could not be built to withstand cannon fire, castles lost their military usefulness; some, such as Windsor Castle, were converted into large houses.

YOUR HEALTH
C
with Dr Kay Hadley

How can I heal all my burns?

Q I cook a lot and am prone to small burns on my hands and wrists. Is there any way that I can soothe these naturally and, perhaps, get them to heal more quickly?
J. Smith, London.

A The most important thing after you have burnt yourself is to run cold water over the burn. This takes much of the heat out of it and helps to limit its severity. For maximum benefit, keep the burn under cold running water for several minutes and apply ice too.

While minor burns can be treated at home, large or severe injuries should be looked at by a doctor, just in case you need medical treatment.

Pure essential oil of lavender can be soothing. Apply it several times a day while the burn is healing. This will help it heal quickly with minimum scarring.

Taking certain nutrients may also help healing. Zinc and vitamin C are probably the most important. I recommend you take 30mg of zinc each day and 1g of vitamin C twice a day to promote skin healing.

◉ Retrieving information

Main ideas

After you have read a text more than once, you should be able to recognise the main concerns in it. Most writers will try to convey their main ideas in specific parts of the text, and in particular ways that you will soon recognise. Writers use the title (if there is one), their opening statements and the concluding statements for this purpose. They use emphasis and repetition and deliberately draw attention to what they consider important in their "message". A useful training for you is to try to write a single short sentence saying what you believe the writer is saying. Use your own words, but write it from the same point of view as the original writer. This helps to concentrate your thoughts on what the writer is really saying – the core of the meaning. You will see that there are supporting ideas and examples, and figurative language, but that at the core, there is a straightforward main idea or concern. This is what the writer is really saying.

When you need to have particular information from a text, or when you are reading in order to answer specific questions, the same method of underlining or highlighting key words and phrases as you read is the most effective way of finding what you are looking for. However, remember that writers often repeat the information, or change it slightly later on, so it's a good idea to read right through and mark areas of the writing where the same, similar or even opposite ideas come up. That way you can see through the writer's system and can put these ideas into your own words. You learn them that way.

To put this into practice, follow these simple steps.

In an exam:

- read through the passage or text first
- don't worry about understanding everything first time
- read through the questions
- read the text again
- note information you now know will form answers
- note what you still have to find
- underline or highlight as you read
- use your own words unless asked to quote or "write down"

! REMEMBER Underlining key words and phrases as you read will help you recall main ideas and specific information from the text when you are writing answers.

This practice piece is a newspaper article. Read it (using the system described opposite) and write answers to the questions.

The Guardian, Monday 6 October 1997

The difference a day made Jazzie B

Jazzie B was born in north London, of Antiguan parentage. He co-founded Soul II Soul in 1982 and now owns a recording studio, record label and fashion line. He lives in London with his partner and two children. Soul II Soul's sixth album, Time for Change, was released last month.

The day was Sunday April 6 1997 – the day my dream came true. Jazzie B playing Wembley in front of 75,000 people – and I scored. It rectifies everything in my life.

In the seventies, when I was at school in Holloway, it was everyone's childhood dream. But you never could really imagine yourself at Wembley coming down the tunnel, never mind scoring more or less from the halfway line and watching the ball go into the net. I used to want to be a PE teacher, because being a football player wasn't something I thought I could do – there were not many black players at that time and my icon was Clyde Best, even though he played for West Ham and I was an Arsenal boy. He was the only one I could really relate to.

I have a big family and as the youngest was treated as a kind of mascot (I was so spoiled as a little kid) and when I scored, everything went through my mind really fast. I remember thinking: "Did it go in?" and then: "Wait till I tell my brothers, they are not going to believe this."

I was playing in a celebrity match before the Coca-Cola Cup final. When I'd got the letter asking me to play, I was running round the studio like a kid. Things like that get me truly excited.

It really was unbelievable. I felt like I did when we had our kids, I was walking on a cloud. It was the winning goal, so they gave me the ball and I had to do a lap of honour and everything. It was mental.

I remember my teachers saying to me: "You must work hard and play hard" and it's true. Put a bit of hard work and belief into something and it becomes a reality; when you lose sight of your belief, it fragments. I've had number one albums, done all sorts of things, but nothing beats playing football at Wembley.

Annie Taylor

1 What is Jazzie B's main idea here?

2 What did Jazzie B want to be when he was at school?

3 Which does he think is better – having a number one album or playing at Wembley?

4 What did he do when he got the letter asking him to play in the celebrity match?

5 What is the name of Soul II Soul's sixth album?

6 Who wrote this article?

7 Find and write down **three pieces** of information about **each** of the following:

■ Jazzie B's job   ■ his childhood   ■ the celebrity football match

Use your own words. Don't copy long pieces of information from the text.

Fact and opinion

Facts are things we can prove and things we know for certain are true. Opinions are personal – they are what a person believes. They may not be the same as other people's views. They may not even be true.

Fact or opinion?

Look at this advertisement (right).

(?) *Is this fact or opinion?*

The use of the number might make you think that it is a fact. But how do we know that the offers are "fantastic"? This is somebody's **opinion.**

Now what about this one (right)? This is a **fact** because the statement can be proved.

(◎) *Look at the key points highlighted in the passage below. As you can see, there are examples of both facts and opinions.*

! REMEMBER Don't be tricked by numbers. They can appear in both facts and opinions.

Easy pickings on the street

Have you ever watched the police moving a car that's causing an obstruction? Or asked for help when you've inadvertently locked yourself out of your car? If so, you'll know just how easy it is for someone who knows what to do, and has the right equipment, to get into your car.

1 — As a part of our car tests we check the security of doors, windows, boot or tailgate, bonnet, glovebox, steering column lock, petrol filler lock and sunroof.

Here we tell you what we've found. It adds up to a sorry picture for car owners and a disgraceful one for car makers.

5 —

6 —

Buying a car is, for many people, the second most costly purchase they make in their life – second only to buying their own home. And yet car makers seem to put car security pretty low on their list of priorities. **2**

3

We can't publicly blow the whistle on the specific design weaknesses we find in doors and locks, for fear of worsening the crime rate. But the makers know the problems as well as we do. They should be making doors more secure, protecting the ignition system and fitting an alarm system as standard (or, at least, offering it as an option). The car makers must take more action to combat the sky-high car crime figures. **4**

1 is a **fact** because this could be checked and proved to be true.

2 is also a **fact** because this could also be checked.

3 is an **opinion** because it is the personal belief of the writer.

4 is also an **opinion** because this is a suggestion and not something which can be checked.

5 and **6** are **opinions** because they refer to feelings or beliefs rather than to known facts.

! REMEMBER Underline key words and phrases in the exam before you decide if they're facts or opinions.

Look out for words which signal opinions such as:

seem   appear   suggest   might   should   could   would

These all suggest possibilities rather than something that can be proven.

Look out for **emotive** words or phrases, such as "it adds up to a **sorry picture** for car owners and a **disgraceful** one for car makers."

These are words which are intended to appeal to your **feelings** or **emotions**. People often use them when they are expressing an opinion.

Points of view

Earlier, you saw that every time you read something, it makes sense to remember that someone wrote it, someone who had a purpose and also had a point of view. Everything is affected by this point of view. Some people think, for example, that the news in the papers or on radio or TV is objective. Yet it has been affected by a point of view. Think of the ways that events are referred to by different newspapers. Think of what they each include in the newspaper. The broadsheets don't usually have pin-up pictures, and the tabloids aren't much interested in the stock exchange or financial markets. How can the same people be referred to as terrorists and as freedom fighters?

Writers of fiction have a point of view also. In the Reading exam, certain questions ask you to show that you can recognise the point of view of the writer. Don't confuse this with simply noticing his opinions on a subject. The writer may just state his opinions straight out. He or she will also have a point of view that you will recognise because of the way he or she sees things and reports them or describes them, and you should be alert for clues to this underlying factor. The use of emotive words, for example, will give you clear clues as to what a writer thinks or feels about a subject. When Liz Lochhead writes in her poem, "Bairnsang",

> Oh,
> saying it was one thing
> but when it came to writing it
> in black and white
> the way it had to be said
> was as if
> you were grown up, posh, male, English and dead

she is commenting on what happened to her good Scots language when she started going to school. Is there any doubt about her point of view? You could take any one of the words in the last line and write quite a long answer on what her view is. Is there any doubt about this writer's (my) point of view in the paragraph you have just read?

This is the kind of questioning approach you should adopt when you are reading any piece of writing. The clues you are looking for are exactly the same as the messages you get when you watch and listen to someone speaking to you. You are probably quite good at reading what we call body language. Have you ever thought why we call it body language? It's the secret, unconscious signs we give to others. We do it in writing also, and reading the signs is one of the ways of finding the author's point of view.

! R E M E M B E R
A fact can be proven. An opinion is a personal belief.

61

Reading

◉ *A simple exercise is to take a short extract from a piece of fiction that you know is written by a man, and see what changes are needed if it were to be written by a woman. Try re-writing it. This is a quick and effective way to recognise what we mean by a point of view.*

◉ Following an argument

Being able to follow an argument is a skill you need in reading, and it is tested in the Reading exam.

Following an argument simply means understanding and explaining the points of view presented in a text.

One writer might argue that the minimum age for legally buying fireworks should be raised because of the rise in firework accidents among young people. To make this argument, the writer might include **facts** about the dangers of fireworks as well as his own **opinion** about the irresponsible behaviour of young people.

❶ REMEMBER Always read the whole text through and underline key words.

How to follow an argument

■ Read the whole passage

■ Underline the key words and phrases which best express the writer's argument

■ Work out the different stages of the argument.

❶ REMEMBER You can check if you understand an argument by seeing if you can tell someone else what the text is about.

Read through the article below. It presents one woman's view about putting her mother into a residential home for old people.

◎ *Underline words and phrases that reveal her different thoughts. List the difficulties she has in arranging care for her mother. Then list the positive results of putting her mother in a home.*

Look out for the turning point in the article: "I started looking at homes..."

Is it fair to put Mum in a home?

Mum is 88, and she'd lived in west London for 53 years before she had a fall in April this year, and was taken into hospital. I'd always worried that if she needed more care, I couldn't cope at home. She needs lots of help, but wouldn't want me to give up my career. It would be impossible for her to live with us – our house is too small.

But all the guilt and the social pressures are horrendous. A lot of people are shocked that I could even think about putting my mother in a home.

Mum hates hospitals, and her mental state was deteriorating when she first went in. She had another fall in hospital, but then she was transferred to a terrific rehabilitation ward.

The social workers there said Mum's needs would be assessed to see what sort of care she required. I was scared she'd need nursing care – a lot of people in nursing homes are very confused, and I was worried that Mum would be put in a room full of mad people.

I started looking at homes, and the one I'm hoping Mum will go to looks excellent. We're still waiting for the final assessment and for the council to agree that this particular home is right for Mum.

Before she had her fall I knew she needed help, but I couldn't persuade her to take it. Now I know she'll be well cared for, her meals will be cooked for her and she'll have people around her, and we've actually become closer as a result of her fall.

In the next example – a report from the *Guardian* newspaper – the writer comments on various points of view related to the changing world.

While this article clearly presents various points of view about the changing world, it also suggests further arguments about:
- the role of the monarchy
- the place of technology
- gender issues and equal opportunities.

Behind every argument, there are often further issues which are not stated directly but are implied. These are known as **implications**. What you do in recognising these implications is to **infer**. You draw **inferences** from the text.

◎ *Read the article and write answers to the questions below.*

Queen, 71, bemoans trials of modern life
Jamie Wilson on varied reactions to the monarch's reflections

She may have her own internet site, and was jetting around the world before most people had ever been airborne, but yesterday the Queen confessed that she found it hard to keep up with the modern world.

The 71-year-old monarch, who is in Pakistan on the second day of her state visit, told the country's parliament: "I sometimes sense that the world is changing almost too fast for its inhabitants, at least for us older ones."

Her comments drew support from a number of her more elderly subjects. Veteran writer and broadcaster Ludovic Kennedy said he agreed entirely: "What she has said is absolutely right. For old dogs like us, new tricks are simply unacceptable."

Mr Kennedy, 77, continued: "The world is changing so fast we just can't keep pace with it.

"That is something older people have to accept."

Romantic novelist Dame Barbara Cartland, 95, echoed the Queen's sentiments, saying: "The world is changing too fast. The Queen is right, we need to get back to the way we were in the past.

"We need to get back to a previous age, where men behaved like gentlemen and women were women and not so busy building their careers. I think that is what the Queen was trying to say and I agree with her."

However, Tony Benn, the 72-year-old Labour MP, felt one change was long overdue.

"The one thing that has not changed in my lifetime is the monarchy. If we could move into the next century with an elected head of state I would feel optimistic," he said.

But it was not all pessimism at the fast rate of progress. Betty Felsted from St Albans, a 70-year-old member of the Women's League of Health and Beauty, said that old people were sometimes blinded by science but that should not stop them from trying to keep up. "Just before I retired I learned how to use a word processor and I have no problem with video recorders or washing machines: I just read the instructions and get on with it.

"I always have a go at anything that comes along."

But Age Concern spokesman Margaret McLellan was sympathetic to the Queen's remarks, saying: "Many elderly people will feel the same way as the Queen.

"Feeling too old to catch up with the modern world can begin when people are as young as 40 or 50, and it is a feeling which gets worse as people get older."

1 What point is the Queen making about modern life?

2 How does Ludovic Kennedy support and extend the Queen's point of view?

3 Look again at Barbara Cartland's views on the changing world. In what ways are her arguments different from those of Ludovic Kennedy?

4 What does Tony Benn's contribution add to the argument?

5 In what way do Betty Felsted's arguments disagree with some of the previous statements?

6 Out of all the views presented in this article, which is the closest to the views of the Queen? Explain why.

Drawing inferences from a text

Not every text will contain implied ideas from the author, but often the writer will not spell out every last detail, and will leave some work for the reader. You might be able to **deduce** things from what the writer says. When you do this, you are **drawing an inference** – finding something that either must be the case, or is probably true, because of what was said, but is itself not stated directly.

⊙ *Look at this piece of writing from F. Scott Fitzgerald's, The Great Gatsby.*

> Turning me around by one arm, he moved a broad flat hand along the front vista, including in its sweep a sunken Italian garden, a half acre of deep, pungent roses, and a snub-nosed motor-boat that bumped the tide offshore.
>
> "It belonged to Demaine, the oil man." He turned me around again, politely and abruptly. "We'll go inside."
>
> We walked through a high hallway into a bright rosy-coloured space, fragilely bound into the house by french windows at either end. The windows were ajar and gleaming white against the fresh grass outside that seemed to grow a little way into the house. A breeze blew through the room, blew curtains in at one end and out the other like pale flags, twisting them up toward the frosted wedding-cake of the ceiling, and then rippled over the wine-coloured rug, making a shadow on it as wind does on the sea.

❓ *What time of year was it?*

As you can see, the writer has not told you directly, but you put two and two together and deduce that because

- the roses were out
- the french windows were wide open
- the grass was fresh
- they were walking in the garden

that it almost certainly was summer.

There are other inferences to be drawn from this short piece from F Scott Fitzgerald's novel of the American jazz age, *The Great Gatsby*. You can probably work out:

BITESIZEenglish

- whether Tom Buchanan (the "he" in the extract) was rich or poor
- whether he was shy or not.

You can also tell something about the narrator's point of view when you look at descriptions like:

frosted wedding-cake of the ceiling

Obviously, he thought the house was over-decorated. He is saying something about taste and the style favoured by the nouveau-riche, those with "new money", as opposed to the "old money" of the wealthy.

At a deeper level, if you knew that the name of the oil man, Demaine, was very close to the French word "demain" meaning "tomorrow", you might draw some kind of inference from that.

There is more than enough here to alert you to look for all the underlying things that any writer might be telling you without saying it all directly and obviously. We take meaning from this kind of writing in the most subtle way. This is one of the valuable skills you are to develop in the course.

 Practise the skill of inference from now on in all your reading, for works you will write about in the Reading part of the folio and in the Reading exam, and for both fiction and non-fiction texts. It involves "reading between the lines", as we say.

Inferences can be about:

- main ideas or particular information
- emotions and feelings of characters
- points of view, opinions and feelings of the writer.

If you can make inferences from the text, you can:

- work out answers from clues or references in the text
- say more based on **connotations** of words in the text
- use your own experience or understanding to match with the text and produce answers where direct information is not in the text.

! **R E M E M B E R**
Whenever you read a text, always look for underlying meaning as well as the obvious meaning.

Identifying the purpose of a text

So far you have looked at literary texts, an advice leaflet, magazine articles and newspaper cuttings. Each text is different depending on its **form**, its **purpose** and its **intended audience**.

REMEMBER Underline key words in the text that will help you to decide its form, purpose and audience.

In order to identify its **form,** you need to ask yourself: what is it? Is it an advertisement, an article, a travel brochure, a diary extract, a poem, a short story or something else?

In order to identify its **purpose,** you need to ask yourself: why was it written? Was it written to inform, explain, instruct, entertain, advise, persuade or for some other reason? Does it have more than one purpose?

In order to identify the **audience,** you need to ask yourself: who was it written for? Was it written for an adult, teenager, child or a combination of these? Was it written for someone with a particular interest? What else can you work out about the intended reader?

If you pay attention in your reading to **form, purpose** and **audience,** your understanding is sure to be improved. When you are writing about literary texts in your folio, and certainly in the Reading exam, questions on these three aspects are going to arise. Trying to decide on these three questions for the text you are reading will actually help you to understand it better.

◎ *Read the pieces of text on the opposite page, then write an answer for each text under the headings below. The first one is done for you.*

	FORM (what is it?)	PURPOSE (why is it written?)	AUDIENCE (who is it written for?)
A	a recipe	to instruct	anyone wanting to cook a quick, cheap meal for one
B			
C			
D			
E			

A

Savoury Eggs   *Serves 1*

A cheap and tasty variation on the bacon 'n' egg theme; makes a good, quick supper.
For a change, cooked, sliced sausages or slices of salami can be used instead of bacon.

Preparation and cooking time: 25 minutes.

1 small onion
1 small eating apple
1 rasher of bacon
2tsp cooking oil or large knob of butter (for frying)
Salt and pepper
¹/₄ tsp sugar
2 eggs

Peel and slice the onion. Wash, core and slice the apple. Derind the bacon and cut into ¹/₂in (1.25cm) pieces. Heat the oil or butter in a frying pan over a moderate heat. Add the bacon, onion and apple, and fry, stirring occasionally, until soft (about 5 minutes). Stir in the salt, pepper and sugar. Remove from the heat. Break the eggs into a cup, one at a time, and pour on top of the onion mixture. Cover the pan with a lid, and cook for a further 3 to 5 minutes over a very low heat, until the eggs are as firm as you like them.

B

OUTREACH PROGRAMME

SSPCA Education Officers speak on a wide variety of topics relating to animal welfare from intensive farming, conservation, pollution and dog problems to general cruelty and the role of the Society as a pressure group. There is no charge.

Booking: Bookings for the Scottish SPCA's six locally-based Education Officers are dealt with centrally. Please contact:

0131 339 0222 (Mon-Fri) for **Edinburgh & East, Glasgow & West**
01224 581236 (Mondays only) for **Aberdeen & North East, Highlands & Islands**

NB Education Officers visit areas systematically to reduce costs. If you give as much notice as possible, we will do our best to meet your needs.

C

IMPORTANT SAFEGUARDS

When using electrical appliances, basic safety precautions should always be followed, including the following:

1. Read all instructions.
2. Do not touch hot surfaces.
3. To protect against electric shock do not immerse cord or plugs in water or other liquids.
4. Do not insert metal objects, knives, forks or similar implements into the bread slot.
5. Close supervision is necessary when any appliance is used by or near children.
6. Do not use any unauthorised attachments with your toaster – they may be hazardous.
7. Unplug from outlet when not in use and before cleaning.
8. Do not cover your toaster whilst it is hot or in use.
9. Appliance should not be used if the supply cable is damaged or dropped causing visible damage.
10. The use of accessory attachments not recommended by the appliance manufacturer may cause injury.
11. Do not use outdoors.
12. Do not let cord hang over edge of table or worktop or touch hot surfaces.
13. Do not use appliance for other than intended use.
14. Bread may burn. Therefore toasters must not be used near or below curtains and other combustible materials. They must be watched.

SAVE THESE INSTRUCTIONS

D

Now she's old enough to look after her own smile – what about yours?

Return to nursing
Full or part-time flexible hours

Giving up a few years to look after a child has its own special rewards. But when they no longer need all of your time, returning to work can be a daunting prospect. Whatever your reason for taking time out, don't worry – your nursing skills are always valuable, whether they were learned 10 months or 10 years ago. If you've had a break from nursing, for however long, we can offer you one of the best ways to get back in.

E

May 1920 Date		hours	
14	repairing waggons	5.35	
	lifting G & S W waggon at Forestmill	4	9.35
15	repairing foot boards of engine 768	3	
	general charges	1.5	4. 05
17	repairing waggons	8.35	8.35
18	repairing waggons with Tool Van at Harbour		
	Alloa engine 271	7	
19	repairing waggons	5.35	
	repairing H R waggon at Alloa	4	9.35
	£3-2-7		
	£4-1-7		
	18		
	£8-2-2		

W Gilmour
10 Brighae
Stirling

How information is presented

You're probably already aware of the different ways the texts we read in our daily lives are presented. You can easily spot the different styles of, say, an advertisement, a recipe, a newspaper report or a drama script.

In the Reading exam, you may be asked to comment on the effect and impact of the appearance, or **layout**, of texts as well as their content. The texts you are asked about in this way will tend to be non-fiction texts.

Headlines

! REMEMBER In the Reading exam, you might be asked to explain how the layout helps you to understand the message of a text.

Newspapers and magazines make use of bold lettering, capital letters and exclamation marks. These make the headline appear dramatic and eyecatching.

DIRTY WATER KILLS!

Have you got what it takes?

In this headline, the question mark gives you something to think about.

The pound sign and the number attract your attention here.

£10 BUYS A CHAIN CUTTER

! REMEMBER Note any changes in the style and size of the print in a text.

Different sorts of print

Often a text will use a range of types of print to draw attention to particular points.

This typed letter opens with a handwritten style. One reason for this is that it tries to make the appeal more personal and direct.

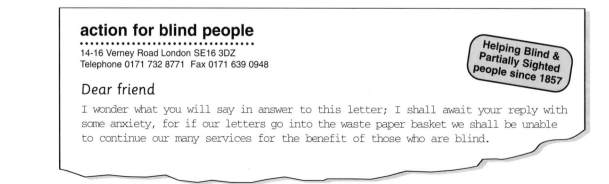

action for blind people
··································
14-16 Verney Road London SE16 3DZ
Telephone 0171 732 8771 Fax 0171 639 0948

Helping Blind & Partially Sighted people since 1857

Dear friend

I wonder what you will say in answer to this letter; I shall await your reply with some anxiety, for if our letters go into the waste paper basket we shall be unable to continue our many services for the benefit of those who are blind.

Logos

Companies and charities use logos as a visual image which you can identify whenever you see them.

BBC RADIO 1

Charts and diagrams

Charts and diagrams are used to present complex information in a simple and easy-to-read way.

◎ *Look in today's newspaper or a recent magazine and see if you can find three charts or diagrams. Think about the impact they have on the reader.*

Photographs and illustrations

Visual images have a powerful impact on the reader. We often look at a picture before we read the text. The way pictures are used can set the tone for a text. For example, cartoons can create a jokey effect, while photographs can add a sense of realism.

◎ *Look at the appeal for Oxfam (below) and write answers to the questions underneath it.*

Oxfam
FREEPOST (OF 353)
274 Banbury Road
Oxford OX2 7BR

Help them build a future free from hunger and disease

How does Oxfam make your £2 work so hard?

How can we possibly make just £2 do so much?

The answer lies in the effort, the determination, and the ingenuity of the people we help.

Oxfam doesn't walk into a Third World country with ready-made solutions, or quick-fix answers. We work alongside local people, and help them work out solutions that suit their individual circumstances.

The projects Oxfam supports are always carefully monitored, so that money isn't wasted, and worthwhile lessons can be applied elsewhere. Oxfam supports 3,000 projects in over 70 countries worldwide.

...for just £2 a month.

**Your £2 a month will help these people in their daily struggle to help themselves.
Please complete the coupon inside.**

---

1 How many different kinds of print (fonts) can you identify?

2 Why do you think the print is of varying sizes?

3 What impact do you think is made by the pictures?

4 Write the copy for "the coupon inside" mentioned in the last line.

Evaluating the language of a text

In the last couple of pages, you looked at the way text is presented. This section will help you to identify some types of language used in texts and comment on them. You are expected to be able to notice and comment on the writer's technique when you read. It is particularly valuable in commenting on how the writer uses language to be able to explain how well it works. Examiners like to ask, "How effective do you think it is?"

Types of language

Dramatic or emotive language

This is used to attract the reader's attention – especially in newspaper headlines. **Emotive** language is language which is intended to arouse strong feelings. In the example (left), the word "crisis" attracts your attention and encourages you to read the article.

Hospitals face crisis over fall in blood supplies

Imperative or directive language

Imperatives and **directives** are words which give us orders or instructions. They are used to appeal directly to the reader and to make the message very clear. In the example (right), the word "discover" is an imperative.

DISCOVER Your FAVOURITE days out in PERTHSHIRE

Alliteration

Ringway rumpus
POLICE were called to Manchester Airport

This is where writers use the same letter to start several words in a phrase, as in the example headline (left). It's another way of catching your attention, this time using **sound** to do so.

Questions

Questions are used by writers to get the reader involved directly. They have the same effect as directives – they make you think the writer is talking to you personally. The article on the next page starts with the question "How green are you?" This has the effect of involving the reader straight away.

◉ *Look at the words underlined in the above paragraph. Notice the mixture of "you" and "the reader" in the same paragraph. You and the reader are the same person. Do they feel the same to you?*

Colloquial language

 R E M E M B E R Make a checklist of types of language to look out for in a text.

This is the name for everyday speech. Colloquial language is informal. It is used to convey ideas in a particular way and to make it easy for the reader to relate to the text. In the text, "How green are you?" on the next page, some examples of colloquial speech have been underlined for you. The whole effect of this text is that of a friend having a conversation with you.

How green are you?

<u>Hands up</u> if you have recently done any of the following:
- thrown a glass bottle in the rubbish bin;
- left the tap running while cleaning your teeth;
- poured cooking oil down the drain;
- flushed cotton wool <u>down the loo;</u>
- left the fridge door open while paying the milkman;
- thrown away plastic carriers from the back of a cupboard;
- heated the oven to bake a solitary <u>spud.</u>

Yes, me too. On the other hand, I do recycle bottles, cans and paper, and take clothes to charity shops, so I thought I was <u>doing</u> pretty well, until I started working on this supplement.

Who can <u>put their hand on their heart</u> and honestly say that they always make the greenest decisions about their home?

◎ *Look through a newspaper or magazine. Find three examples of alliteration, emotive and colloquial language. Find the same more easily in a poem, a novel or a dramatic script.*

Friday October 24, 1997

Community News

....

Ninja peril of Black Lake
Dumped terrapins decimate wildlife

An exotic pet which grows from the dimensions of a 50p piece into a plate-sized monster is causing havoc among wildlife after being dumped illegally in a Wilmslow pool.

There are thought to be dozens of American reared terrapins – left-overs of the Ninja Mutant Turtle craze – in Black Lake on Lindow Common.

The 12in-diameter creatures gobble up insects, newts, frogs and even baby water birds. Experts say that unless the terrapins can be curbed local wildlife will be devastated.

The problem began when the terrapins were dumped after they became too big to handle in household aquariums.

The wily reptiles are proving difficult to catch. So far, they have dodged all efforts at trapping.

The terrapins – *trachemys scripta elegans* – have found the lake in the 43-acre wildlife reserve of scientific and special interest an ideal breeding ground. Even in their native North America, where they are known as red-eared sliders, they are a major problem, producing up to 23 eggs a year.

Macclesfield council countryside officer Richard Doran says anyone dumping the reptiles in the lake can be fined up to £5,000.

"Everything was all right until the Mutant Ninja craze came along," he said.

---

1 Find and underline all the examples of emotive and colloquial language you can in the text above.

2 Mark three examples of where the writer has used language to attract and keep the reader's attention. Write a short note on each one to explain what it is and how it works on the reader.

Collating material

Collating material means gathering together information from different texts. You will not be asked to do this in an exam at Standard Grade, though you certainly will at Higher Grade. It is included here because gathering information for report writing is an important reading skill.

Normally, you would be expected to gather material from a range of texts. We're using only one here.

Study the following text about animal rescue.

(?) *What do you learn about the work of the Scottish SPCA from the appeal?*

(◎) *List six points about the work of the Scottish SPCA, using the phrases underlined in the text to help you.*

The first point is done for you as an example:

"The Scottish SPCA is Scotland's oldest and largest animal charity."

The Scottish SPCA

The Scottish SPCA is Scotland's oldest and largest animal charity, caring for all Scottish animals – pets, farm animals and wildlife. Our Inspectors respond to over 13,000 calls from the public every year; and fourteen Animal Welfare Centres care for almost 18,000 cruelly-treated, injured and abandoned animals. Our Education Department provides a fully integrated educational programme in schools and the wider community; and we campaign in the UK and Europe to improve animal welfare legislation. By joining the Scottish SPCA you can give us vital financial help.

Together, we can improve the lives of millions of animals.

Membership

Over 30,000 people throughout Scotland support the Society. Those who are members receive the bi-monthly Scottish SPCA News – a lively magazine with features and news about animal welfare at home and abroad, and details of our campaigns.

Types of membership

• **Life Fellowship** is available to anyone, 16 years or over, who makes a donation of £275 or more to the Society.

• **Joint Membership** is open to any two persons, both 16 years or over and living at the same address, who jointly subscribe £25 annually.

• **Membership** is open to anyone, 16 years or over, who subscribes £15 annually.

• **Junior Membership** is open to children up to the age of 18, and costs £2 a year. Please contact headquarters for a special Junior Membership application form.

Branches

Voluntary branches throughout Scotland hold a host of fundraising events, from coffee mornings and gift stalls to dances and sponsored dog walks. These events also offer new members the chance to get together with others, and to learn more about the Society.

To get in touch with your local Branch, and if you live in the north or east of Scotland, call Harold Bowron on 0131 339 0222. For Glasgow or the west, call Una Glenn on 0141 810 8084.

The Scottish SPCA ...caring for Scotland's animals

Prevention at work

Today, in Scotland, thousands of living creatures are at risk. Any animal can be made to suffer through the neglect, ignorance, carelessness or deliberate cruelty of human beings.

People abandon dogs and cats in sheds, flats and empty houses, leaving them to starve.

Horses spend winters in barren fields, with no shelter. Farmers let their cattle, sheep and pigs die in fields and filthy byres, leaving disease and injury untreated. Children – and adults – take pleasure in baiting or tormenting captive animals, from hamsters and kittens to rabbits, hedgehogs and foxes.

◎ *Study these texts about endangered species and the problems they face.*

Adoption Papers

NAME: *Kinyanjui*   AGE: *13*   SEX: *Male*

Adopt a rhino, before it's too late

Kinyanjui is a black rhino. Not so long ago – only as far back as the seventies – he would have been one of 60,000 in Africa. Now, a monstrous trade has decimated these numbers. A staggering 95% of black rhinos have been cold-bloodedly butchered for their horns – worth three times the price of gold on the black market. Today, Kinyanjui is one of only 434 of these magnificent beasts left alive in Kenya.

A grim picture? In fact, Kinyanjui and his fellow black rhinos are on the increase, thanks to WWF. Since we began supporting the Kenya Wildlife Service project in 1992, the population has actually risen. But the numbers are still desperately low – which is why we need your help.

Stop the slaughter, adopt Kinyanjui for yourself or a friend

By adopting Kinyanjui for just £2 a month you can help us protect him from the horrors of illegal poaching. To thank you, we'll send you a Certificate of Adoption, a photograph of Kinyanjui and regular updates on his progress. If you could find it in your heart to adopt this remarkable animal you'd be helping us to save more than his life alone. You'll be supporting our goal to see 600 healthy black rhinos in Kenya by the turn of the century, and you'll be helping us to ensure that every endangered rhino throughout Africa and Asia stands a chance of staying alive. The future of rhinos everywhere could depend on you.

£17.50 ADOPT A HUMPBACK WHALE
and protect them 365 days a year.

ACT NOW
A TRULY
HUMANITARIAN GIFT

When you adopt one whale you'll be helping all whales.

Humpback Whales are extremely susceptible to the hazards of whaling, hunting, fishermen and natural calamities such as being beached in their annual migration between Canada and the Caribbean. Many of our female whales that are up for adoption are mothers that have had several babies. You can choose to adopt one of these female humpback whales with her baby for just £17.50 per adoption. Or you can choose a single female or a strong male. The choice is yours.

Whatever you decide upon, you can be certain in the knowledge that your money will be spent directly on the protection and survival of these magnificent gentle giants.

❗ R E M E M B E R
Underline the key points as you study the texts.

◎ *In preparation for report writing later, try these activities. Write your responses objectively. Look at the opening sentences above for help. In a report, you would omit the examples and illustrations you see in the above texts.*

1 What problems do endangered species face? List six points using both texts.

Here's the first point for you:

"The number of black rhinos in Africa has been greatly reduced – in the seventies there were 60,000 black rhinos in Africa."

2 What similarities are there in how the two advertisements have been written? List four points using both texts.

Over your two years studying the Standard Grade course, you'll complete many different kinds of writing. Near the end of the course, some pieces will be selected and sent off to SQA in your folio, and finally you'll have to choose one kind of writing only and show how well you can do it in the Writing exam.

Purposes

Each piece of writing you do will be based on one of the four purposes of Writing. These are:

W1
- to convey information

- to deploy ideas, expound, argue, evaluate

W2
- to describe personal experience, express feelings and reactions

- to employ specific literary forms (for example, short story, letter, poem)

To meet these purposes, you will be asked to do different kinds of writing.

Skills

No matter what kind of writing you tackle, you need these same basic skills:

- plan your work so that your writing is well organised

- direct your writing to your audience

- be aware of your clear purpose in writing

- convey your meaning clearly

- arrange your ideas in sentences and paragraphs

- vary sentences appropriately and adopt suitable style

- use a range of vocabulary

- spell and punctuate correctly.

Planning

REMEMBER It only takes a few minutes to make a plan, but it will improve the quality of your work because you have thought carefully before writing.

You really do have to sit and think first about what you are going to write. It must be well-structured and in logical order. Decide now that everything you write will be planned before you start to write. Write down your plan in note form and stick to it. Think about the purpose first. The task itself will make the purpose clear to you. Decide what you are going to say, how you are going to say it, and in what order. Keep your plan simple – a few key words or phrases will help you to organise your ideas. Think of your plan as always having an introduction, a body and a conclusion.

Audience and purpose

Before you can write anything well, you have to be clear about who is going to read it and why you are writing it. Much of what you do in school is pretending to be doing real things such as writing a newspaper article. You know that it isn't going to be published, but you write it as if it were. Seeing the real purpose is the same. The writing task will always point to a purpose.

Paragraphs

Dividing your ideas into paragraphs is essential for the reader following your argument or story. A paragraph contains your ideas on the same topic, all in the same place. Stop and read your work every few minutes and this will help you to see where one set of ideas, or one idea, ends and another begins. Sentences usually deal with a single idea, with some information that modifies it. Reading aloud what you have written is one of the simplest ways to recognise what should be in your sentence. Vary the sentence types that you use and remember to make them clear and stylish.

Punctuation

Punctuation is a system of marks to tell the reader how to read what you have written. It is a convention that you must keep to, even though not everybody has always used it. It is difficult to separate punctuation from other matters such as sentence construction. Reading aloud can help with punctuation. You must master the use of basic punctuation marks, particularly the full stop. You should also be able to use correctly the comma, the colon, the semi-colon, inverted commas, exclamation and question marks, the dash and the hyphen. If you don't already know how to use these, ask your teacher for a book containing exercises so that you can practise. Wide reading helps too (books, not newspapers).

Spelling

For your written work for the folio, you have plenty of time to re-draft your work, and that includes getting all the spelling correct. The best guide to spelling is wide reading, but there are spell-checkers and spelling guides too. In the Writing exam, you won't have these aids with you, but careful checking of your work can remove an amazing number of mistakes. When in doubt about spelling, writing down the word and variants can help, but only if you are familiar with the word written down.

⑦ *Can you see which is correct: language or langauge?*

Writing

In class and for your folio, you can write by hand, or you can use a word-processor to present your work and make it legible (easy to read). In the exam, remember that the examiners must be able to read your handwriting or they can't assess your ideas or award any grade.

❗ REMEMBER Read through your work after you have written each paragraph. That way you are more likely to spot mistakes and avoid repeating yourself.

❗ REMEMBER Punctuation is the only criterion, by itself, that can fail your work.

Writing

Forms of writing

It doesn't make any difference to the form of writing whether you are producing a piece of writing in the class or the exam, but there are one or two differences about how you should work. There is more about this on pages 87-8.

You can see that the purposes set out earlier cover a range of different kinds of writing. There are four purposes but these break down into two main purpose types: **transactional** and **expressive**.

In Standard Grade, they are called W1 and W2 (W is for Writing).

Roughly, the first two deal with factual writing (but not always); the second two deal with more creative writing (but include writing about your own experiences). Within these broad purposes, there are quite a few different forms of writing. The forms of writing you might be asked to attempt could include:

Transactional	Expressive
■ newspaper report	■ short story
■ magazine article	■ script
■ discursive writing	■ descriptive writing
■ informative writing	■ diary/journal
■ business letter	■ reflective/personal writing
■ persuasive writing	■ poem

The essential thing is that your writing shows that you are aware of the purpose. This means that you have to recognise from the task what kind of writing you are supposed to produce (form) and also what you are writing for (purpose). There is a link between the form and the purpose in most cases. If you are asked to write a news report for a newspaper, for example, you should set it out as in a newspaper and make sure it is conveying information. Writing an account of your holiday won't do instead. While it's close in purpose (conveying information), it isn't close in form. The examiners mark what has been asked for: other pieces are irrelevant and inappropriate in an assessment situation. While your teacher can do something about this in class work, examiners cannot in exam work. So, always study the task very carefully, and get both purpose and form right.

 REMEMBER Use facts to inform your reader, use 'you' to address the reader and ask questions to involve him or her.

Transactional writing

Newspaper report

Newspaper reports tell readers about events that have been happening locally, nationally or internationally. You will usually be asked to write about local events. The purpose is to convey information. The reader should receive the information quickly and easily, so reports should be straightforward, using concrete language and a crisp style. Think of the summary statement at the start of the report – it catches the reader's attention and contains the gist of the story. Typical openings are shown below.

Jailed Robber Plea

The parents of a Scot jailed in America for bank robbery have appealed to the prison authorities to let him complete his sentence in Scotland.

Two In Hospital After Crash

TWO people were taken to hospital after a crash involving three cars and a van in Marionville Road, Edinburgh, last night.

The report needs planning as all writing does. The plan here is a list of questions. Imagine them coming from your potential readers: who?, what?, where?, when?, why?, how?

◎ *Pick up a newspaper now and read the first article you find that deals with an accident. See how it answers these questions. Use a marker to circle the information and then in the circle write the question it is answering – who? what? etc.*

If the article has been well written, it will deal with them all. Notice that the "what?" question is often answered first, as in the examples above, and then again later.

Notice also that there is a headline to grab your attention. There will usually be a short paragraph to answer each of the questions. These will be short and sharp with clear and concise information. Articles of this kind have to be concise. They need to be redrafted and then edited by other people (sub-editors). Direct speech is used as is indirect speech. It is always written in the past tense, of course, since it reports events that have taken place. It is set out in columns.

◎ *Take a news report from your local paper and rewrite it, changing all the names, places, events and quotations. Keep exactly the same order and structure, however. You'll be surprised to see how easy it is to understand how this kind of writing works.*

◎ *When you have done that, write a report of your own about a fire in a house near where you live. Nobody was killed or injured, but there were narrow escapes and a heroic rescue.*

Articles that are not news reports have different rules. Articles can be discursive, informative or persuasive.

Writing

Articles can cover a wide range of topics depending on the audience and the purpose of the publication in which they appear. Some articles are written to give advice. Others are written to inform the reader.

Articles don't always simply report news. They can also be written to develop an argument or to present a particular point of view.

◎ *Read the examples on this page and the next and decide in each case who is the audience and what is the purpose.*

■ You can see that articles adopt a different tone according to the audience.

■ The vocabulary of the first text is informal, while the writer of the second text uses a few technical terms and facts and figures.

■ The distinguishing features of article writing are labelled for you on page 79.

Hi-tech, low life

Do computers turn children into spotty, uncommunicative youths? Not always
says **Bill O'Neill**

Your seven-year-old daughter is determined to prove that she's now big enough to be a nerd, too. She slips into the back room while the rest of the family is watching Blind Date, switches on the computer and keys in the password (cleverly stuck on the back of the machine so children won't find it).

You're not worried about her coming across an unsolicited invitation among your family e-mail to surf the Internet in search of a "hot new product, try me out", the sort of appeal that thinly disguises a new pornography site; you cancelled your subscription to the company that provided your connection to the Internet more than a month ago because the service was too expensive and getting on-line too unpredictable.

No, your real concern these days is the amount of time that the children spend in front of that damn machine; they seem to be at it all day in school, and then want to do the same in the evenings and at the weekends at home. It'll ruin their eyesight, make them even more uncommunicative than they already are and generally turn them into fat, spotty youths, fit only to be wrapped in an anorak.

How come no one else realises that computers are designed to appeal to the lazy streak, that's why children like using them so much? Don't give me all that guff about improved motor skills and budding entrepreneurs – it's games, games, games. Once a child has made it to the terminal, everything he or she needs to pass the time of day is just a finger tap away, without having to move. On the computer, you're in charge; and if things don't go your way, you can simply press the re-set button.

issue identified in first paragraph

headline designed to catch interest of audience – here it uses humour

opinion of expert

opinion of expert

use of facts and figures

range of views given

Writing

Gee Mom, TV has made me American

By Sean Poulter
Media Correspondent

Children are watching so many American television programmes they are losing touch with British life, a watchdog warned yesterday.

Some have such a constant diet of Stateside shows that they believe 911 – the US emergency number – rather than 999 is the one to call in a crisis.

As well as alienating youngsters from their own culture, American TV does not instil the social values British programmes do, said Jocelyn Hay, from the voluntary watchdog Voice of the Listener and Viewer.

Home-grown shows are more likely to get children thinking about and acting on social issues, she told the group's conference in London. 'With American TV, what we are also losing is the social and educational values linked with British television, such as the children showing compassion and interest in other parts of the world,' she added. 'For instance, when they see something on Rwanda, they go back to school and have a jumble sale.'

An invasion of cartoon characters is also squeezing out high-quality children's drama and educational programmes.

Since 1981, cartoons on BBC and ITV have jumped from 10 per cent to around 33 per cent of programming. Yesterday, broadcasters were warned that the 'dumbing down' of children's programmes would eventually filter into general schedules.

Anna Home, who has just stepped down from running the BBC's children's output, said it is becoming harder to get good-quality children's drama on screen. Miss Home, who commissioned the controversial Teletubbies, said 'High-quality drama is under pressure because it is so very expensive.'

The conference heard that children prefer series such as EastEnders, Casualty and Friends to those specifically aimed at them.

At the same time, critics complained that violent cartoons shown on ITV on Saturday mornings – and other programmes such as the Power Rangers – are becoming dominant.

The squeeze on quality programmes was confirmed by the Broadcasting Standards Commission. Director of research Andrea Millwood-Hargrave said the explosion of satellite channels has unleashed a tide of American cartoons. There are now five satellite children's channels. As a result, programming aimed at youngsters has risen from 10,000 minutes in 1991 to 86,000 minutes in 1996.

ITV's Michael Forte said parents should take a bigger role in directing children's viewing. 'Cartoons are great, but not a solid diet,' he added.

Discursive writing

This kind of writing isn't "discussive" – it has to do with discourse rather than discussion. It requires you to deal with a topic and use ideas and argument. An example is a piece of writing on the use of animals in medical research. You have ideas and there is a case to be argued:

- for the idea
- against the idea
- a balanced view

This is one of the more difficult options, and is often not very successfully done in the exam or the folio. These are the basic requirements:

- begin with planning (as always)
- knowledge and information on the topic
- an interest in the subject
- a clear view
- a formal tone.

Planning

First, draw up a plan for your essay. There will be:

- an introduction in which you bring the matter to the reader's attention, say what you intend to deal with, and state your view of the matter

- a succession of paragraphs introducing your ideas on the topic in logical sequence, and building your argument

- a conclusion in which you make clear where you finally stand and claim that you have presented your case fairly and convincingly.

Researching

Research the topic properly, using sources available to you: reference works, library sources, discussion with knowledgeable persons, CD-ROMs and, perhaps, the Internet, press, TV or radio.

Learn the facts and then write in your own words.

Writing

Discursive writing is best attempted for your folio rather than in the exam because of what is involved.

The writing in a discursive essay must be formal, not colloquial slang or spoken language. The formality is closely linked with the purpose and form. The prose should be in continuous sentences, in paragraphs. If you plan carefully, your ideas will build up into a case that your reader should find convincing, or at least worth considering. Although you are not simply conveying information, by the end you should have given your reader much information on the topic, backed up by supporting reasons, and in this way, made clear what is your stance on the topic.

80 **WARNING!** Do not even attempt to write discursively if you don't know much about the subject.

WARNING! Gathering and using information does **not** mean simply copying it from the sources without having learned it for yourself. Copying someone else's words is plagiarism, and is completely unacceptable to the examiners. In fact, it can lead to your certificate being cancelled.

Informative writing

One of the most obvious writing tasks in purpose 1 – conveying information – is to write an essay which provides the reader with information. There is the question of what the information is about, of course. It could be about a hobby or interest of yours, it could be about some event, place or object; it could be about a topic such as welding or aerobics.

Generally speaking, this conveying of information in an informative essay will deal with factual matters. Expressive and creative writing are dealt with later (page 83).

Planning, researching and writing

Everything already said about planning in connection with discursive writing applies to this form as well. The research is very similar as well. It is the use to which the material is put that is different. You will not be deploying ideas or presenting an argument for the reader to consider. You will simply be providing the reader with useful information. It has to be interestingly presented, of course, for otherwise it will have failed to be successful writing. People don't read what doesn't interest them. This fact should remind you to choose a subject that is interesting to you. You are then much more likely to make it interesting.

Since this form of writing has so much in common with discursive writing, it is not a good choice in the exam unless you choose to write about something with which you are completely familiar, almost an expert. It's best kept for the folio and for class work, when you have adequate time and access to information sources. Strictly speaking, it's not your knowledge of the subject that is being tested, but it is very difficult to produce good writing if you don't have material to write about.

When you come to write

- Use your notes and plan.
- Decide the best order for your information.
- Use clear paragraphs.
- Use sentences of varied type.
- Think about effective word choice.
- Check how you express your ideas.
- Use link words from paragraph to paragraph.
- Check your work and amend.

! WARNING! While this form of writing could be about yourself, it should not be confused with other purposes, such as reflecting on personal experience.

! WARNING! The warning about plagiarism is repeated. Don't just copy information from other sources. The skill that is being assessed here is WRITING, not copying.

ON-LINE There isn't space to deal with all the forms of transactional writing, but there is much more about this in the on-line guide. Look it up! See page 7 for the address.

Writing

Persuasive writing

Read the text below which was written to persuade people to visit the New Lanark Visitor Centre. The text mixes some facts with lots of opinions and uses carefully chosen words to persuade the reader that this is a good place to go. Some of these words have been underlined for you. See how many more you can find.

New Lanark Today

Today, as you wander around the village, it is easy to imagine how people lived and worked two centuries ago. New Lanark has been beautifully restored as a living, working community where visitors are welcome.

In the Visitor Centre there's a truly fascinating trip back in time called the 'Annie McLeod Experience'. Suddenly it's 1820, and the 'ghost' of young Annie, a mill girl of that time, is introducing you to her world. It's a chair ride, twisting and turning through history itself, with a surprise around every corner. Children love it!

Next you can see and hear the awesome machinery of the Industrial Revolution, a memorable insight into life in a textile mill. Working demonstrations will show you that, despite Owen's humane attitudes, life on the mill floor was never a picnic.

In the Millworkers' House you can see what life was like in the 1820s with 'hurlie beds', or in the 1930s 'room and kitchen' with its new-fangled electric light and 'stairheid cludgie'.

In Robert Owen's House, with its Georgian-style furnished rooms, you can discover more about the life and times of the social pioneer and his radical ideas about society. Find out how he wrote himself into the history books!

And remember: if you're looking for budget-priced accommodation, there's one of Scotland's finest Youth Hostels right in the heart of New Lanark – in a former millworkers' row. Behind the historic exterior is amazingly comfortable accommodation and a warm welcome. Self-catering facilities or home-cooked meals are available.

NEW LANARK
VISITOR CENTRE

❗ REMEMBER
When writing to persuade, include lots of emotive language to make your description more exciting. Emotive language will also help you to make your point more directly.

Expressive writing

This kind of writing includes the creative writing that you know well: the short story, poem, drama script, the fiction journal/diary and much descriptive writing. It also includes writing about personal experiences and the reflective writing that can arise from this.

Personal experience

Of all of the types of expressive writing mentioned above, writing that describes personal experience is by far the most popular, and according to the examiners, the most consistently successful in both the folio and the exam. A commonly set task requires an account or description of some experience that you have had. This might seem to be an easy option, but this is still about writing: it's not just about remembering. Converting experience into writing needs the same planning, research, organisation and actual writing before it succeeds.

Planning, researching, organising and writing

All writing starts with planning and making notes. You may be fed up hearing this, but don't ignore it; your writing will suffer. Even though the subject is your own life, and you are the expert in that subject, you should think about what you are writing for. Think also about the central ideas. Think about the best order for what you want to say.

The order in which things happened is not necessarily the best way of telling a story. Organise the events into a sequence of paragraphs. Depending on the specific purpose set out in the task, you may have to present things in a particular way, and come to a particular kind of conclusion.

You must still pay heed to the way you express your ideas and information.

Almost certainly, the task or assignment will require you not only to describe your experience, but also to say what you felt about it at the time and, often, to reflect upon that experience now. It involves not just telling a story, but considering the following:

- how did you feel?
- what did you think?
- what do you think about it all now?
- what have you learned from that experience?
- what advice do you think you would give to others?

This reflecting or thinking back is not something that you add on at the end. It should be part of your planned writing. This kind of writing, provided you follow the same system of planning, is one that you can tackle quite effectively in the exam as well as in your class work. One additional thing to note is that it is the kind of writing in which you can really express your

Writing

feelings, ideas and experiences. For that reason, it tends to lead to strong, sincere, convincing writing. However, it also deals with an area of your life that you might want to keep partly to yourself. You might not want to write about it for your teacher to read. The good thing about the exam is that the examiner has no idea who you are, and is interested only in the quality of the writing. So, overall, this kind of writing is a good exam choice.

Short story

The short story is a work of fiction in prose. It is short compared to most novels, but could be quite long. In the exam, you are limited by time, of course. In the folio, you are expected to submit writing of reasonable length. There is no actual limit – it should be appropriate to the (literary) form.

The story will be made up, but could be based on real events. Stories have certain basic requirements:

- characters
- plot
- dialogue
- point of view
- setting
- description

The short story takes characters at a particular point and deals with a significant moment. It doesn't have many characters, doesn't cover a long time span and doesn't involve lots of complex issues. There is no such thing as the standard short story, but there are certain guidelines.

The best way to learn what a short story is like is by wide reading. Short stories are easily available in collections and your teacher can recommend some. Read several stories by different writers. Reading stories by the same author will give you an idea of the type that a writer prefers, and helps you to analyse the structure of the stories.

Here are some brief pointers for writing stories of your own.

Characters

The short story writer doesn't tell the reader directly about the characters. Words, thoughts and actions reveal them. Look at the section on drawing inferences (pages 64-5). This is where you use it for writing. There should be very few characters – no more than three.

Point of view

Once you have a character or characters, decide on the point of view for the story. It has to be told in the first or third person – "I" as the storyteller, or "he/she". If it's "I", think carefully about which "I" in the story tells it, for it will decide the whole story. Using the first person allows you to let the character reveal things about himself/herself by thinking aloud and reacting to others and events. Using the third person allows you to be more objective. The choice is important and it should be the best one for the story. Try changing the point of view of a short story you are reading and you will quickly get the point.

Plot

There has to be an event: something must happen. It does not have to be a momentous or even very important thing on the face of it, but it should be central to the story because it affects the character(s).

Setting

The setting is where the story takes place and helps greatly to make it convincing. You can use description, dialogue and details to make the setting work well. It's likely to be effective if you choose a familiar setting.

Setting your story in Khufaifiya in Saudi Arabia if you have never been there and live in Auchterteuchty is less likely to be effective.

Dialogue

Characters live when they speak. Dialogue should always sound right. Say it aloud to make sure it does. The words the characters speak reveal their personalities. Keep it short, though. Use inverted commas and a new paragraph for each speaker.

 Look at a short story to check how dialogue is set down on the page and use this layout when you write.

Description

Use description when there is a point, not just to break up the dialogue. Describing weather and scenery can advance the mood and tone of the story. Describing the character is a way of revealing him/her (in a third person approach).

Start and finish

Your opening must catch the reader. Dialogue, description, or reflection can do this.

Endings are important in short stories. Often they leave us for a moment thinking it's not the end. Then we think about it and see the point. The writer is not hammering home the ideas, but helping us to arrive. It should never try to sum up "what happened after that". The ending doesn't have to have a surprise built into it, especially the one that tells the examiner that it was all a dream – that very predictable and boring ending!

Writing

Drama script

A drama is intended to be performed and this fact affects the form of writing. It has to be written in such a way that it sounds effective when it is performed on stage, in a film, or on TV or radio.

Form

The writing consists of dialogue to be spoken by the characters and stage directions for those who are to act and direct. The narrative and the characterisation have to be contained in the dialogue and directions. There is no other way that the writer can tell the reader anything.

 The form is easy to recognise. Study the layout in a drama text. You'll see that the name of the character is written on the left, usually in capital letters: stage directions are written in brackets, or sometimes in italics. The dialogue to be spoken is written beside the name of the character.

Character

The first thing again is that you should plan your writing before you begin and keep to your plan. A short drama script of the kind you might write for your folio or in the exam should have few characters, so that you can develop each one a little. A cast of thousands means cardboard characters. Characters come alive through the dialogue so make it sound real. As for the short story writing, say it out loud to test it.

Plot

A drama usually has some crisis, conflict or issue at the centre. The characters are to react in this situation and this is what makes the centre of the action. As for the short story, the issue need not be earth-shattering or unusual. Look at how simple the problems of the soap operas really are: a misunderstanding, an argument about groceries or the loss of a cat. It is the way it is handled and how the characters behave in the story that counts.

Whatever the plot, it should be able to work on stage. A script that called for the sinking of the Titanic on stage would not be rated successful.

Dialogue

Dialogue is most important. It has to be convincing, and that means really thinking about the characters who are to speak it, the age, the kind of person, the mood, the listener(s). All of these things affect how we speak. Where we come from is important too, as is our accent and the tone we use in the situation (angry, excited, frightened, formal or informal).

Reading and Writing in the exam

Reading

You'll sit two levels of exam in Reading, 50 minutes each, with a break between them. In each, there will be a passage, probably prose but not necessarily; it could be a poem or an extract from a play and there may be illustrations, headlines and other graphic material as well. It might be fiction or non-fiction.

The passage will normally be printed at A3 size (about the size of two pages of this book), and there will be a separate question/answer booklet.

Remember to use the reading system discussed earlier:

- start by reading the information on the question paper
- read the passage, underlining as you go
- read the questions
- read the passage again, checking off against questions
- write answers, carefully noting what is asked for
- check your work.

Tips

The Reading paper has a number of standard question forms, a kind of code almost.

- When it asks you to <u>write down (quote)</u>, use the word(s) of the passage.

- When it asks for <u>your own words</u>, make sure that you use your own.

- When it uses **bold type** like this, pay attention to the specific words: they often specify the **number of words or reasons.** Giving the wrong number means you lose marks.

- When it asks <u>why do you think</u>, it means say what <u>you</u> think. Remember to give a reason.

- <u>Explain as fully as you can</u> means that you must write a fairly extensive answer if you want to gain full marks.

- <u>Look at paragraph 7</u> means that the answers to the questions that follow are in paragraph 7. Don't use any information from paragraph 10, because it will be the wrong information.

- The space and/or number of lines printed after the question is designed to give you an idea of the kind/length of answer. It is assumed that your writing is of average size. If there are four lines, don't write just a few words. It won't be enough for full marks. This is important. Most pupils lose marks not because they get the answers to some questions wrong, but because they don't give full answers to the ones they get partly right.

- Some questions have more than one part. Make sure that you attempt all the parts, because if you don't, you'll lose marks.

- Many questions ask you to give a reason for your answer. You must notice these questions. This is very important because the reason is worth more than the answer!

- Sometimes, you will find a sneaky "Why?" after the main question. Again, the answer to that is worth as much or more than the earlier part of the question.

Writing

What you've read earlier in the Writing Skills section applies broadly to your writing in the class, whether or not it is going to end up in your folio. It also covers most of the writing in the exam, but there are one or two other points you should consider.

The first and obvious thing is that you will be writing within a strict time limit. You will have no support materials of any kind with you. You won't be able to re-draft in the full way that you can for class work. You will have just the exam paper, your pen, your ideas and the skills you have been learning and practising for the two years of the Standard Grade course. These are more than enough. You know what to do, so don't panic. You can do it.

The question paper in the Writing exam is quite user-friendly. It is inviting you to choose one kind of writing, to consider its clear purpose (from the assignment), to think about the question and your ideas, and to look at the stimulus material. This could be either text, photographs or other graphics.

There is a wide choice of about 24 assignments, many of them with alternatives within them. You are to write one single piece. It will be completely familiar in form and the purpose will be clear from the rubric (the instructions about what to do).

You will have an hour and fifteen minutes to do all the work, so

- read the assignment and choose ONE
- read the instructions and look at the photograph, if there is one
- think about purpose and ideas
- write your plan
- write the essay/letter/script/article/story you choose
- keep an eye on the time: don't try to write until the last minute
- take up to ten minutes to read over your work and correct it
- read it once more... and smile.

Practice exam papers

No exam papers are printed here because there are better ways for you to see real exam papers and use them.

■ Your teacher will probably have copies of the Writing papers in school, since schools and colleges are allowed to keep the question papers after the exam. He or she may be willing to let you see these: but maybe not.

■ Unfortunately, your teacher will not have the Reading papers, apart from the Text (the separate A3 passage) because obviously the question/answer booklets are sent back to the SQA at Dalkeith.

■ You can buy your own individual copies of the question papers from the SQA's agents. They are:

Robert Gibson, Publisher
17 Fitzroy Place
Glasgow
G3 7SF

They will give you information and prices if you write to the above address or telephone 0141 248 5674. Books containing sets of papers from the previous four years or so are also available from the same source.

■ It's a good idea to see real exam papers before you ever sit the exam. Being prepared includes knowing what to expect. You should expect the unexpected however. Do not assume that the exam you sit will be exactly the same as the past papers you see. They follow a general plan, but there is scope for variation from year to year.

Digging by Seamus Heaney

Between my finger and my thumb
The squat pen rests; snug as a gun.

Under my window, a clean rasping sound
When the spade sinks into gravelly ground;
My father, digging. I look down

Till his straining rump among the flowerbeds
Bends low, comes up twenty years away
Stooping in rhythm through potato drills
Where he was digging.

The coarse boot nestled on the lug, the shaft
Against the inside knee was levered firmly.
He rooted out tall tops, buried the bright edge deep
To scatter new potatoes that we picked
Loving their cool hardness in our hands.

By God, the old man could handle a spade.
Just like his old man.

My grandfather cut more turf in a day
Than any other man on Toner's bog.
Once I carried him milk in a bottle
Corked sloppily with paper. He straightened up
To drink it then fell to right away.

Nicking and slicing neatly, heaving sods
Over his shoulder, going down and down
For the good turf. Digging.

The cold smell of potato mould, the squelch and slap
Of soggy peat, the curt cuts of an edge
Through living roots awaken in my head.
But I've no spade to follow men like them.

Between my finger and my thumb
The squat pen rests
I'll dig with it.

The Early Purges by Seamus Heaney

I was six when I first saw kittens drown
Dan Taggart pitched them, 'the scraggy wee shits',
Into a bucket; a frail metal sound,

Soft paws scraping like mad. But their tiny din
Was soon soused. They were slung on the snout
Of the pump and the water pumped in.

'Sure isn't it better for them now?' Dan said.
Like wet gloves they bobbed and shone till he sluiced
Them out on the dunghill, glossy and dead.

Suddenly frightened, for days I sadly hung
Round the yard, watching the three sogged remains
Turn mealy and crisp as old summer dung

Until I forgot them. But the fear came back
When Dan trapped big rats, snared rabbits, shot crows
Or, with a sickening tug, pulled old hen's necks.

Still, living displaces false sentiments
And now, when shrill pups are prodded to drown
I just shrug, 'Bloody pups'. It makes sense:

'Prevention of cruelty' talk cuts ice in town
Where they consider death unnatural,
But on well-run farms pests have to be kept down.

Mid-term Break by Seamus Heaney

I sat all morning in the college sick bay
Counting bells knelling classes to a close,
At two o'clock our neighbours drove me home.

In the porch I met my father crying –
He had always taken funerals in his stride –
And Big Jim Evans saying it was a hard blow.

The baby cooed and laughed and rocked the pram
When I came in, and I was embarrassed
By old men standing up to shake my hand

And tell me they were "sorry for my trouble",
Whispers informed strangers I was the eldest,
Away at school, as my mother held my hand

In hers and coughed out angry tearless sighs.
At ten o'clock the ambulance arrived
With the corpse, stanched and bandaged by the nurses.

Next morning I went up into the room. Snowdrops
And candles soothed the bedside; I saw him
For the first time in six weeks. Paler now,

Wearing a poppy bruise on his left temple,
He lay in the four foot box as in a cot.
No gaudy scars, the bumper knocked him clear.

A four foot box, a foot for every year.

Follower by Seamus Heaney

My father worked with a horse-plough,
His shoulders globed like a full sail strung
Between the shafts and the furrow.
The horse strained at his clicking tongue.

An expert. He would set the wing
And fit the bright-pointed sock.
The sod rolled over without breaking.
At the headrig, with a single pluck

Of reins, the sweating team turned round
And back into the land. His eye
Narrowed and angled at the ground,
Mapping the furrow exactly.

I stumbled in his hob-nailed wake,
Fell sometimes on the polished sod:
Sometimes he rode me on his back
Dipping and rising to his plod.

I wanted to grow up and plough,
To close one eye, stiffen my arm.
All I ever did was follow
In his broad shadow around the farm.

I was a nuisance, tripping, falling,
Yapping always. But today
It is my father who keeps stumbling
Behind me, and will not go away.

Storm on the Island by Seamus Heaney

We are prepared: we build our houses squat,
Sink walls in rock and roof them with good slate.
The wizened earth has never troubled us
With hay, so, as you can see, there are no stacks
Or stocks that can be lost. Nor are there trees
Which might prove company when it blows full
Blast: you know what I mean – leaves and branches
Can raise a tragic chorus in a gale
So that you can listen to the thing you fear
Forgetting that it pummels your house too.
But there are no trees, no natural shelter.
You might think that the sea is company,
Exploding comfortably down on the cliffs
But no: when it begins, the flung spray hits
The very windows, spits like a tame cat
Turned savage. We just sit tight while the wind dives
And strafes invisibly. Space is a salvo.
We are bombarded by the empty air.
Strange, it is a huge nothing we fear.

The Choosing by Liz Lochhead

We were first equal Mary and I
with same coloured ribbons in mouse-coloured hair
and with equal shyness,
we curtseyed to the lady councillor
for copies of Collins' Children's Classics.
First equal, equally proud.

Best friends too Mary and I
a common bond in being cleverest (equal)
in our small school's small class.
I remember
the competition for top desk
or to read aloud the lesson
at school service.
And my terrible fear
of her superiority at sums.

I remember the housing scheme

where we both stayed.
The same houses, different homes,
where the choices were made.

I don't know exactly why they moved,
but anyway they went.
Something about a three-apartment
and a cheaper rent.
But from the top deck of the high-school bus
I'd glimpse among the others on the corner
Mary's father, mufflered, contrasting strangely
with the elegant greyhounds by his side.
He didn't believe in high school education,
especially for girls,
or in forking out for uniforms.

Ten years later on a Saturday –
I am coming from the library –
sitting near me on the bus,
Mary
with a husband who is tall,
curly haired, has eyes
for no one else but Mary.

Her arms are round the full-shaped vase
that is her body.
Oh, you can see where the attraction lies
in Mary's life –
not that I envy her, really.

And I am coming from the library
with my arms full of books.
I think of those prizes that were ours for the taking
and wonder when the choices got made
we don't remember making.

Kidspoem/Bairnsang by Liz Lochhead

It wis January
and a gey dreich day
the first day I went to the school
so
ma Mum happed me up in ma good navyblue nap coat
wi the rid tartan hood
birled a scarf aroon ma neck
pu'ed on ma pixie and ma pawkies
it wis that bitter
said
'noo ye'll no starve'
gied me a wee kiss and a kidoan skelp on the bum
and sent me off across the playground
to the place I'd learn to say
'It was January
and a really dismal day
the first day I went to school
so
my Mother wrapped me up in my best navyblue top coat

with the red tartan hood
twirled a scarf around my neck
pulled on my bobble-hat and mittens
it was so bitterly cold
said
"now you won't freeze to death"
give me a little kiss and a pretend slap on the bottom
and sent me off across the playground
to the place I'd learn to forget to say
"It wis January
and a gey dreich day
the first day I went to the school
so
ma Mum happed me up in ma good navyblue nap coat
wi the rid tartan hood
birled a scarf aroon ma neck
pu'ed on ma pixie and ma pawkies
it was that bitter."

Oh,
saying it was one thing
but when it came to writing it
in black and white
the way it had to be said
was as if
you were grown up, posh, male, English and dead.

Box Room by Liz Lochhead

First the welcoming. Smiles all round. A space
For handshakes. Then she put me in my place –
(Oh, with concern for my comfort). 'This room
Was always his – when he comes home
It's here for him. Unless of course,' she said,
'He brings a Friend,' She smiled 'I hope the bed
Is soft enough? He'll make do tonight
In the lounge on the put-u-up. All right
for a night or two. Once or twice before
He's slept there. It'll all be fine I'm sure –
Next door if you want to wash your face.'
Leaving me 'peace to unpack' she goes. My weekend case
(Lightweight, glossy, made of some synthetic
Miracle) and I are left alone in her pathetic
Shrine to your lost boyhood. She must
Think she can brush off time with dust
From model aeroplanes. I laugh it off in self defence.
Who have come for a weekend to state my permanence.

Peace to unpack – but I found none
In this spare room which once contained you. (Dun-
Coloured walls, one small window which used to frame
Your old horizons). What can I blame
For my unrest, insomnia? Persistent fear
Elbows me, embedded deeply here
In an outgrown bed. (Narrow, but no narrower
Than the single bed we sometimes share).

On every side you grin gilt edged from long-discarded
selves
(But where do I fit into the picture?) Your bookshelves
Are crowded with previous prizes, a selection
Of plots grown thin. Your egg collection
Shatters me – that now you have no interest
In. (You just took one from each, you never wrecked a nest,
You said). Invited guest among abandoned objects, my
position
Is precarious, closeted so – it's dark, your past a
premonition
I can't close my eyes to. I shiver despite
The electric blanket and the deceptive mildness of the
night.

Peace by Rupert Brooke

Now, God be thanked Who has matched us with His hour,
And caught our youth, and wakened us from sleeping,
With hand made sure, clear eye, and sharpened power,
To turn, as swimmers into cleanness leaping,
Glad from a world grown old and cold and weary,
Leave the sick hearts that honour could not move,
And half-men, and their dirty songs and dreary,
And all the little emptiness of love!

Oh! we, who have known shame, we have found release there,
Where there's no ill, no grief, but sleep has mending.
Naught broken save this body, lost but breath;
Nothing to shake the laughing heart's long peace there
But only agony, and that has ending;
And the worst friend and enemy is but Death.

The Soldier by Rupert Brooke

If I should die, think only this of me:
That there's some corner of a foreign field
That is for ever England. There shall be
In that rich earth a richer dust concealed:
A dust whom England bore, shaped, made aware,
Gave, once, her flowers to love, her ways to roam,
A body of England's, breathing English air,
Washed by the rivers, blest by suns of home.

And think, this heart, all evil shed away,
A pulse in the eternal mind, no less
Gives somewhere back the thoughts by England given:
Her sights and sounds; dream happy as her day;
And laughter, learnt of friends, and gentleness,
In hearts at peace, under an English heaven.

Attack by Siegfried Sassoon

At dawn the ridge emerges massed and dun
In the wild purple of the glow'ring sun,
Smouldering through spouts of drifting smoke that shroud
The menacing scarred slope; and, one by one,
Tanks creep and topple forward to the wire.
The barrage roars and lifts. Then, clumsily bowed
With bombs and guns and shovels and battle-gear,
Men jostle and climb to meet the bristling fire.
Lines of grey, muttering faces, masked with fear,
They leave their trenches, going over the top,
While time ticks blank and busy on their wrists,
And hope, with furtive eyes and grappling fists,
Flounders in mud. O Jesus, make it stop!

Dulce et Decorum est by Wilfred Owen

Bent double, like old beggars under sacks,
Knock-kneed, coughing like hags, we cursed through sludge,
Till on the haunting flares we turned our backs
And towards our distant rest began to trudge.
Men marched asleep. Many had lost their boots,
But limped on, blood-shod. All went lame; all blind;
Drunk with fatigue; deaf even to the hoots
Of gas-shells dropping softly behind.

Gas! GAS! Quick, boys! – An ecstasy of fumbling,
Fitting the clumsy helmets just in time,
But someone still was yelling out and stumbling
And flound'ring like a man in fire or lime...
Dim, through the misty panes and thick green light,
As under a green sea, I saw him drowning.

In all my dreams, before my helpless sight,
He plunges at me, guttering, choking, drowning.

If in some smothering dreams you too could pace
Behind the wagon that we flung him in,
And watch the white eyes writhing in his face,
His hanging face, like a devil's sick of sin;
If you could hear, at every jolt, the blood
Come gargling from the froth-corrupted lungs,
Obscene as cancer, bitter as the cud
Of vile, incurable sores on innocent tongues –
My friend, you would not tell with such high zest
To children ardent for some desperate glory,
The old Lie: Dulce et decorum est
Pro patria mori.

Strange Meeting by Wilfred Owen

It seemed that out of battle I escaped
Down some profound dull tunnel, long since scooped
Through granites which Titanic wars had groined.

Yet also there encumbered sleepers groaned,
Too fast in thought or death to be bestirred.
Then, as I probed them, one sprang up, and stared
With piteous recognition in fixed eyes,
Lifting distressful hands, as if to bless.
And by his smile, I knew that sullen hall,
By his dead smile I knew we stood in Hell.

With a thousand pains that vision's face was grained;
yet no blood reached there from the upper ground,
And no guns thumped, or down the flues made moan.
'Strange friend,' I said, 'here is no cause to mourn.'
'None,' said the other, 'save the undone years,
The hopelessness. Whatever hope is yours,
Was my life also: I went hunting wild
After the wildest beauty in the world,
Which lies not calm in eyes, or braided hair,
But mocks the steady running of the hour,
And if it grieves, grieves richlier than here.
For of my glee might many men have laughed,
And of my weeping something had been left,
Which must die now. I mean the truth untold,
The pity of war, the pity war distilled.
Now men will go content with what we spoiled.
Or, discontent, boil bloody, and be spilled.
They will be swift with swiftness of the tigress.
None will break ranks, though nations trek from progress.
Courage was mine, and I had mystery,
Wisdom was mine, and I had mastery;
To miss the march of this retreating world
Into vain citadels that are not walled.
Then, when much blood had clogged their chariot wheels.
I would go up and wash them from sweet wells
Even with truths that lie too deep for taint.
I would have poured my spirit without stint
But not through wounds; not on the cess of war.
Foreheads of men have bled where no wounds were.

'I am the enemy you killed, my friend.
I knew you in this dark: for so you frowned
Yesterday through me as you jabbed and killed.
I parried; but my hands were loath and cold.
Let us sleep now...'

Suggested answers

These answers are for the Reading Skills section only. The questions about writing and literary texts often ask for your own ideas or opinions, so there isn't any one answer. If you want to check your progress on these type of questions, you could ask your teacher to look at your answers.

Reading skills (page 57)

Text A: a leaflet written to explain how to vote.
Text B: an encyclopedia entry to give information on castles.
Text C: an extract from a questions and answers letters page in a women's magazine.

Retrieving information (page 58-9)

Jazzie B
1 playing at Wembley was an important event in his life
2 Jazzie B wanted to be a PE teacher
3 playing at Wembley
4 he ran round the studio like a kid
5 Time for Change
6 Annie Taylor and Jazzie B
7 *Facts about Jazzie B's job:* he co-founded Soul II Soul in 1982; he now owns a recording studio, record label and fashion line; his sixth album was released last month.
Facts about Jazzie B's childhood: he went to school in Holloway; he was the youngest in a large family; he was spoiled when he was young; he wanted to be a PE teacher; his hero was Clive Best; he supported Arsenal.
Facts about the celebrity football match: it was played before the Coca-Cola Cup final; the date was 6 April 1997; there were 75,000 people there; he scored the winning goal.

Following an argument and drawing inferences (page 62-3)

Is it fair to put Mum in a home?
Difficulties: social pressure, people were shocked; Mum hates hospitals; her mental state was deteriorating.
Positive results: the home she will go to looks excellent; she will be well cared for; she will have all her meals cooked for her; she will have people around her; mother and daughter have become closer.

Queen, 71, bemoans trials of modern life
1 The Queen says it is hard for an older person to keep up with the modern world.
2 Ludovic Kennedy says it's difficult for old people to adapt to the fast pace of change in the modern world.
3 Barbara Cartland says we need to go back to the ways of the past.
4 Tony Benn questions whether a monarch is needed in the modern world.
5 Betty Felsted is 70 and does not have any problems in keeping up with the modern world.
6 Ludovic Kennedy, because he says "What she has said is absolutely right".

Identifying the purpose of a text (page 67)

B. Form: information leaflet to schools/teachers; written to convey information about support from SSPCA education service.
C. Form: toaster instructions; written to instruct; audience: anyone using the toaster.
D. Form: advertisement; written to persuade; audience: parents who might return to nursing.
E. Form: workman's timesheet; written to convey/record information to supervisor/manager.

How information is presented (page 69)

Oxfam appeal
1 Three different fonts are used.
2 Type size varies to draw attention to different pieces of text.
3 Picture of the children makes reader want to help; picture of pound coins helps emphasise how little money is needed to help.

Evaluating the language of a text (page 71)

Ninja peril of Black Lake
1 Emotive language: peril, decimate, monster, havoc, devastate and colloquial language: dumped, dodged, craze, gobble up.
2 The writer uses various types of language, e.g. emotive (*peril, devastate*), colloquial (*gobble up*) to involve the reader. She/he uses factual language to inform the reader (*producing up to 23 eggs a year*). The direct speech at the end of the article also attracts the reader's attention.

Collating material (page 73)

Endangered species
1 95% of black rhinos have been killed; rhinos are killed for their horns; 434 rhinos are left in Kenya; humpback whales are threatened by whaling, hunting, fishermen and natural calamities; they can be beached during migration.
2 Both adverts give the reader facts explaining why animals are in danger; both make a suggestion of adoption as a gift; both address the reader directly; both use emotive language (*calamities, monstrous*).

Glossary

Alliteration
repeating consonants which sound the same at the beginning of words or stressed syllables. *Example: Peter Piper picked a peck of pickled peppers.*

Argument
the meaning a writer wants to convey in a piece of writing

Assonance
giving the impression that words sound similar by repeating the same or similar vowel sounds with different consonants, or the same or similar consonants with different vowel sounds. *Example: marrows and carrots in furrows.*

Brainstorming
writing down all the various possible meanings and interpretations you can think of after reading a particular piece of writing

Colloquialism
an informal word, phrase or piece of English you might use when chatting. *Example: "spud" instead of "potato".*

Concrete language
specific and definite language, not abstract or figurative

Context
the text which surrounds a word or phrase. A word may fit into its context or may appear to surprise you and be out of context

Convention
a general agreement about how we will do things, an accepted system

Critical evaluation
in Standard Grade, a piece of writing about a work of literature which comments on its content, style, form, technique etc.

Cross-referencing
reading or writing about the different works of an author or authors to point out similarities in content and/or types of expression

Dialogue
conversation between characters

Effect
the impression made on the reader by the writer's use of particular words, expressions or techniques of writing

Emotive language
words or phrases which arouse an emotional response in the reader. *Example: the poor, defenceless animals.*

Expressive writing
the kind of writing that conveys thoughts and feelings

Figurative language or figures of speech
where the meaning of a particular expression isn't the same as the literal meaning of the words. *Example: she was over the moon with joy.*

Foregrounding/highlighting
when the author begins consecutive sentences or lines of verse with the same words or structure

Imagery/images
descriptive words or ideas in a piece of writing

Imaginative response to literature
in Standard Grade, a piece of writing in which the writer attempts to show an appreciation and understanding of a piece of literature by reproducing the style, technique, plot etc. of the original

Inference
what you work out for yourself about meaning, tone etc. from the ideas or statements made (by what is implied) by a writer

Irony
using language to express the opposite to what you mean or feel

Jargon
words or expressions used by a particular group or profession. The meaning is therefore often unknown to "outsiders"

Metaphor
describing something by saying it is another thing (cf simile). *Example: he's a wizard at Maths.*

Narrative method/style
how the author tells a story in a piece of writing

Objective language
not affected by personal feelings, emotions or points of view

Paradox
a statement that appears to contradict itself. *Example: fair is foul and foul is fair.*

Para-rhyme

words placed at the ends of lines whose consonants are the same or similar but whose vowels are different. *Example: sock/pluck (Heaney's "Follower").*

Personification

giving things or ideas human characteristics. *Example: the hot fat spat in the pan.*

PQD (Point-Quotation-Development)

the system of responding to a work of literature suggested in this book (see page 51)

Propaganda

material which is written or broadcast to persuade the audience to think in a particular way or follow a certain course of action. When the First World War started, for example, the government issued propaganda (leaflets, articles, posters, radio broadcasts, etc.) to persuade everyone to join the war effort

Prose

a form of writing which is not in verse and which doesn't rhyme. Novels and newspapers are written in prose

Rhyme

using pairs or groups of words, usually at the end of lines of verse, which have the same or very similar sounds

Rhyme scheme

used to discuss the way a poem rhymes. Write A to denote the sound of the last word of the first line. If the second line ends with the same sound, write A again. If it's different, write B. Do the same thing with all the lines in the poem. You might find that the rhyme scheme of a poem with three four-line stanzas is AABB, or ABAB, or ABCA, etc.

Rhyming couplet

two consecutive lines of verse which rhyme with each other, and are usually about the same length. If the rhyme scheme of a poem is AABBCC and so on, the poem is written in rhyming couplets

Rhythm

a term usually applied to poetry, but which can also be used for drama and prose. Rhythm is produced by the stress given to words when they are read aloud. If the stress falls on words at regular intervals, this is called regular rhythm. If the stress falls with no particular pattern, this is called irregular rhythm

Rubric

the directions or instructions as to what you have to do (in an exam question, for example)

Simile

describing something by saying it is *like* or *as* something else (cf metaphor). *Example: I've been working like a dog.*

Soliloquy

a speech spoken by an actor alone on stage, designed to reveal the character's innermost thoughts and feelings

Sonnet

a poem containing fourteen lines

SQA

Scottish Qualifications Authority (formerly Scottish Examinations Board and Scotvec)

Stanza

a poem is usually divided into lines grouped together called stanzas. Hymn books call them verses, but use the word *stanza* in poetry

Symbol

a word which describes one thing, but also stands for something else. Blake's rose is both a flower and a representation or symbol of love. Many poets use their personal symbols again and again

Texture

the pattern of rhythm and sound in a poem. A piece of material has a texture built up by the threads used to make it and the way it is woven. Poetry has a texture too, made by the words used and the way they are used

Transactional writing

writing whose purpose is to get something done. The opposite of "expressive/creative"

Verse

a term applied to poetic writing, not prose. Note that a verse (singular) is a single line of a poem

Word association

using words whose meaning can be used to suggest another meaning. The word red, for example, means a colour, but it can also suggest danger or a political belief